A–Z OF WHITBY

Places - People - History

Ian Thompson and Roger Frost

AMBERLEY

Also by the Authors

Thompson, Ian & Roger Frost, *Secret Whitby*
Thompson, Ian, *Dracula's Whitby*

First published 2020

Amberley Publishing
The Hill, Stroud, Gloucestershire, GL5 4EP
www.amberley-books.com

ISBN 978 1 4456 9306 4 (print)
ISBN 978 1 4456 9307 1 (ebook)

British Library Cataloguing in Publication Data.
A catalogue record for this book is available from the British Library.

Typesetting by Aura Technology and Software Services, India. Printed in Great Britain.

Contents

Introduction

Whitby is one of the most picturesque and interesting towns in England. It is an old fishing and whaling port situated on Yorkshire's Heritage Coast where the River Esk, the only salmon fishing river in the north-east of England, meets the North Sea. It does so through the towering cliffs on either side of Whitby's natural harbour, the largest between the Tyne and the Humber.

The town has a fine mixture of property. It ranges from the ruins of the great medieval abbey, in its commanding position high above the Old Town, to town houses from the same era, Georgian property and fine Victorian houses, especially the unfinished Crescent on the West Cliff.

One of the most striking features of the Whitby landscape are the bright red roofs of many of its buildings. Much of eastern England's coastal roofs are made of similar pantiles, but here in Whitby they seem to glow in the sunlight of summer days. They add a warm, welcoming feeling, which is undisturbed in the cold and rain of winter.

Spectacular as Whitby's location is, it is not this alone which attracts the visitor. Whitby is a place to escape to, a place in which to forget the troubles of our modern

Whitby has been the destination of many holidaymakers for generations.

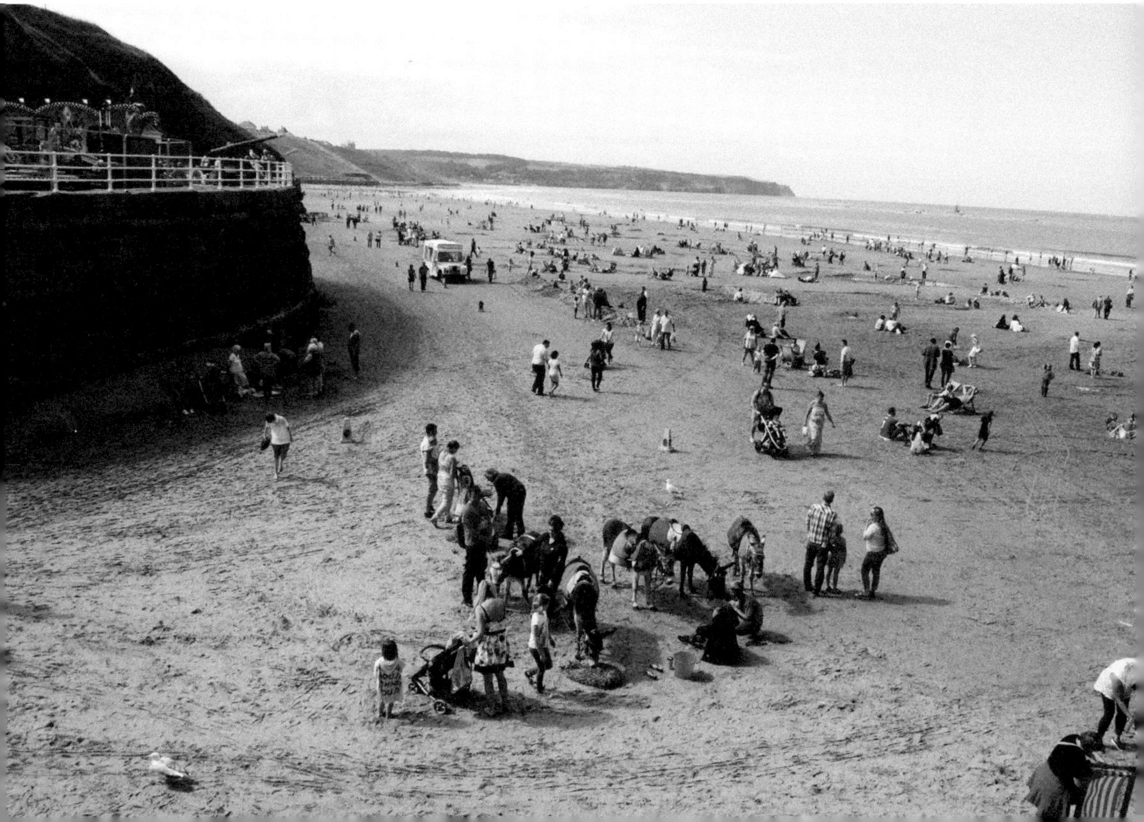

world and seek out solace, not only in the mythical past (something at which Whitby excels) but also in a historic past, one which is deep and enduring.

On the top of the East Cliff, 200 feet above the sea, are the dark ruins of the church of the Norman Benedictine Abbey of Whitby. It was refounded, in 1077, on the site of St Hilda's Celtic Abbey of AD 657. This was the location of the great Synod of Whitby, the first significant meeting of the early English church, which impacts on us today as it settled, at the Synod of 664, the means by which Easter was determined.

St Hilda's reputation for holiness and wisdom established Whitby as a place of pilgrimage, which extended into the Norman and later medieval periods. This was a factor in the development of the town, which grew up not only under the protection of the monks, but also that of the massive East Cliff. It was there that the first settlement was established, and it is in this part of Whitby that many of the town's interesting locations can be found. However, it was the magnificent harbour that provided the impetus for Whitby's development as a centre of trade and industry. Whitby became a small fishing community, small because the town was cut off, by land, from the centres of population that might, otherwise, have provided Whitby with its market.

Whitby's isolated location was something of a problem, but the harbour, protected from North Sea storms, soon developed a host of industries which, over the years, changed the town dramatically. Ship and boat building were always important, and Whitby enjoyed a long history in the coastal coal trade. This plied between the Tyne and Wear and the great city of London, which demanded increasing supplies of coal for its burgeoning population. What made Whitby's coal trade remarkable is that the town had no coal of its own! It was the harbour that came to the rescue. Its waters provided safety for most vessels in a storm, including those carrying the coal. However, the little colliers, many of them locally constructed 'Whitby Cats', built in the self-same harbour, also found protection there. These colliers were some of the finest sailing ships ever made. Captain James Cook, the famous explorer who undertook his

Whitby Abbey is an iconic building that can be seen from sea or land. Now in ruins, the abbey loses none of its majesty.

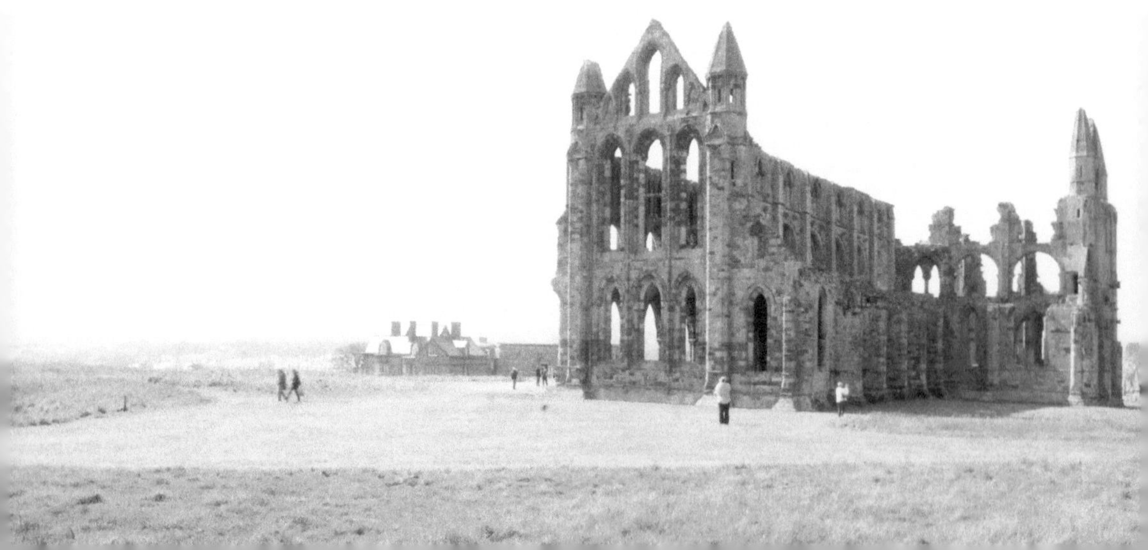

naval training in Whitby, insisted on their use on his famous worldwide voyages. The house where Cook lived, in his Whitby days, is now a museum in his memory and well worth a visit.

Though Whitby remained a town of fishermen, 'collier ships' and shipbuilding, another great industry, emerged in the eighteenth century. Whaling started in a small way but the town became the centre of the British whaling industry in an age when there was vast demand for the products made from the whale, many of which were processed in Whitby harbour.

Today we think that whaling was a cruel industry, not only to the whales but also to the hardy seamen who worked in it. In those days the blubber from the whale could be 'melted' down into oil, which was much in demand as lubrication in the early mills of the Industrial Revolution. Whale oil was also made into soap, margarine, paint and candles and was used in street lighting before gas lamps were invented. Similarly, the skin of the whale was worked into leather, its cartilage made into glue.

The great whale jaw monument on the West Cliff is a reminder of those days of derring-do, but there is little left in Whitby today of its whaling past. Had the industry still been active, not many of you would have wanted to visit the harbour, as the smell from the whale boilers was particularly offensive.

But of course, Whitby is no longer an industrial town. Hints of its industrial past are to be seen everywhere, but the building of the railways, in the 1840s, changed the town for ever. Though Whitby was hardly the quickest town to harness the power of the 'iron horse', the steam locomotive proved to be the town's saviour.

Whitby became a holiday resort welcoming one and all, but it was more than that. The town was a place visited by writers. In fact, Whitby is the cradle of English literature, the home of our first poet, Caedmon. But Bram Stoker (the creator of

Looking back along the pier to Whitby. The town is still a thriving fishing town but also caters for the thousands of tourists who visit each year.

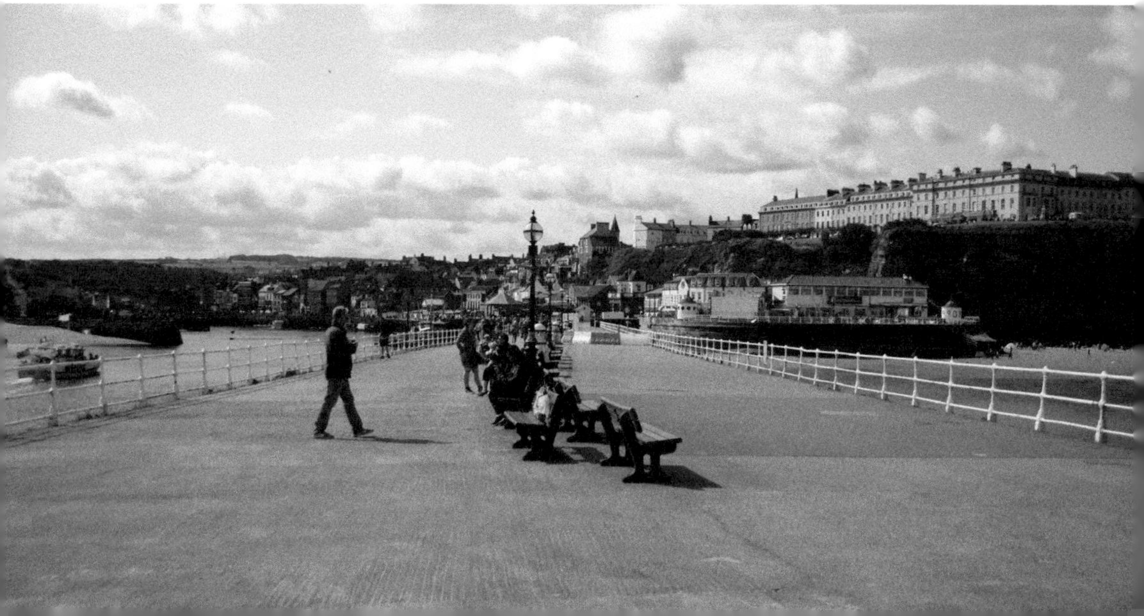

Dracula), Elizabeth Gaskell, Charles Dickens and Lewis Carroll all came here. They were all inspired by the place, but who would have thought that Whitby's associations with Dracula would have brought so many fashionable young people so regularly to the town? Goths, with their black-dyed hair and garish fashions, come to Whitby in great numbers twice a year, to liven-up the place a bit – not that Whitby needs all that much of that!

Whitby is a place of secrets and surprises and these are what make the town such a great place to visit. Someone new to Whitby never quite knows what he is going to see, or hear, next. The town has all the facilities that you will ever need, so it is good for its proud residents too. Enjoy your time in Whitby. There is no other place quite like it.

Roger Frost and Ian Thompson, 2019

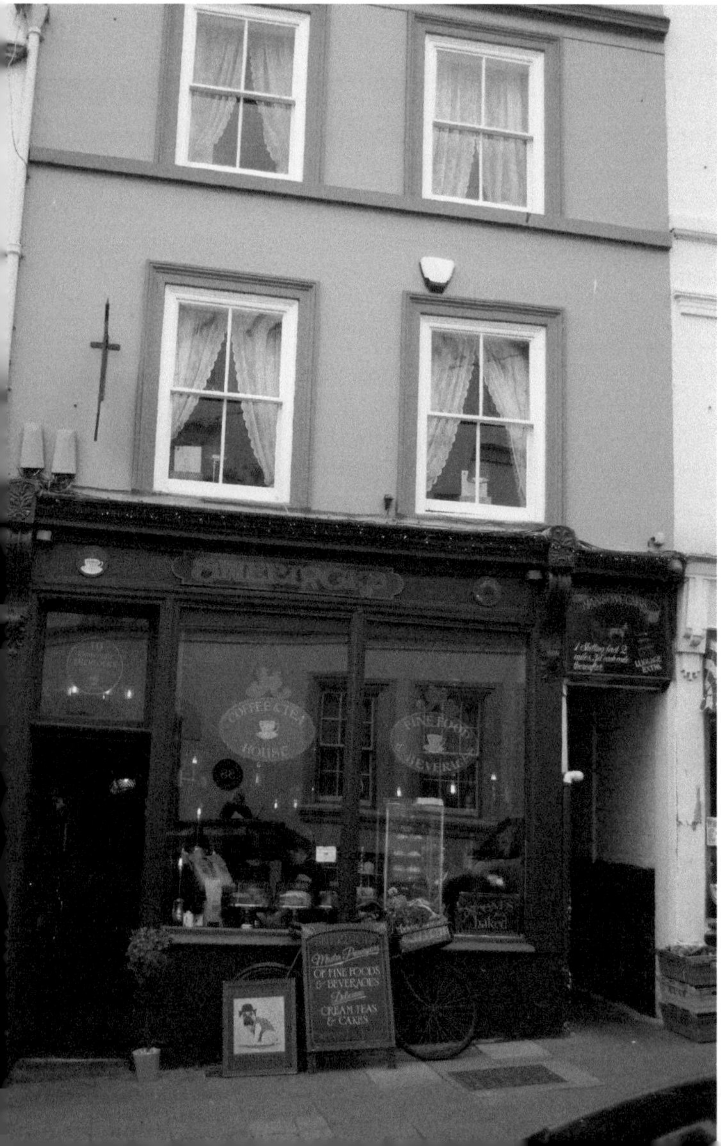

There are many places to find refreshments in Whitby. Sherlocks Coffee House takes you back in time to the Victorian era.

A

Abbey

It seems only fitting that we start our A to Z of Whitby with the landmark that defines the town so well. Perched on top of the East Cliff, with a commanding view of the town, river, and North Sea, Whitby Abbey is one of the most impressive sights in Yorkshire and has been a part of the town since it was founded in around AD 657 by the Northumbrian King Oswy. He appointed Lady Hilda as the Abbess, and the monastery was home to both monks and nuns. The poet Caedmon was also resident at Whitby Abbey. In 664, Whitby Abbey was the setting for the Synod of Whitby when various religious questions were resolved, including the setting of the date of Easter.

The ruins you see today are not the original abbey from the time of St Hilda. They date back to shortly after the Norman Conquest when a Benedictine abbey was founded by one of William the Conqueror's soldiers, turned monk. His name was Reinfrid and he approached the local landowner, William de Percy, for somewhere to build a monastery. De Percy gave him the site of St Hilda's old monastery and the abbey was constructed. It was a successful seat of learning for almost 500 years until it was destroyed in 1540 under the orders of Henry VIII during the Dissolution of the Monasteries.

There has been an abbey on this site since 657. The current abbey is Benedictine and fell into ruin following the Dissolution of the Monasteries.

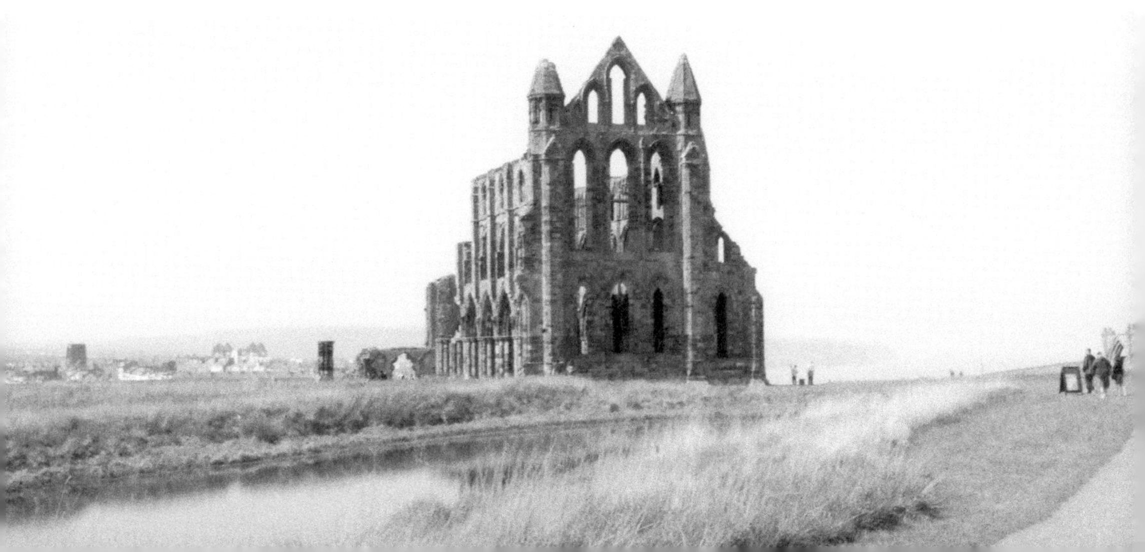

The ruins of the abbey have occupied their place on the clifftop ever since. They have served as a navigation aid for travellers, especially those at sea. The abbey was damaged during shelling by German battleships, during the First World War, as they tried to knock out the nearby coastguard station. Today the abbey is owned and maintained by English Heritage.
See also: Caedmon, Easter, Hilda, World War One Raid

Alum

Alum is a chemical compound, a hydrated double sulphate salt of aluminium, which is combined with potassium to form potassium alum, which, it may surprise you to learn, is a part of our everyday life. It exists in water purification chemicals, leather tanning, dyeing agents for paper and wool, fireproof textiles, deodorant, baking powder, play dough, and shaving products – where the astringent qualities of alum make it a key component of a styptic pencil.

Alum was vital for England's textile trade, where it was used in the dyeing process in the wool industry. At first alum was imported from the Middle East and then, from the fifteenth century, it came from the Papal States. Dyed wool was one of England's biggest industries and alum was vital for this but, when Henry VIII left the Catholic church, in 1534, the imports of alum ceased. This meant that a local solution had to be found.

At the end of the sixteenth century, Sir Thomas Chaloner, of nearby Guisborough, had travelled to the Papal States, in Italy, to view the alum works there. Upon his return, his cousin (also called Thomas) realised that the plants that grew around the family estate were the same as those that grew in areas that yielded alum. Thomas (the cousin) believed that those plants thrived on the minerals that made up alum and so the family, secretly, brought back alum workers from the Papal States and started their own alum works just outside of Whitby.

The results were very successful and they allowed England to become self-sufficient in the production of alum and, subsequently, the country banned its import from abroad. Under James I, the alum works were seized by the Crown but, under royal control, they became a thriving business, as did the English wool industry.
See also: Ammonites, Fossils, Industry, Jet

Ammonites

Ammonites feature on Whitby's coat of arms. Ammonites (or ammonoids to give them their correct name) are extinct marine molluscs. With their distinctive head and tentacles, they resemble octopi or squid; however, the ammonite had a spiral chambered shell with each chamber progressively bigger than the last.

Ammonites first appeared in the Devonian era (nearly 419 million years ago) and disappeared in the Cretaceous-Paleogene extinction event 66 million years ago. Today their fossils can be found beneath the cliffs of Whitby.

Of course, ammonite fossils are not just restricted to Whitby; they can be found all over the world. So, what makes ammonites special to Whitby? Legend has it that Whitby had become plagued with snakes and the inhabitants of Whitby came to the abbey to ask Saint Hilda for help. Saint Hilda first prayed that their heads would fall off and then prayed further that the snakes be turned to stone. This tale is recounted in Walter Scott's epic poem 'Marmion':

They told how, in their convent cell,
A Saxon Princess once did dwell,
The lovely Edelfled;
And how a thousand snakes, each one
Was changed into a coil of stone
When Holy Hilda prayed;

Such was this legend that Victorian entrepreneurs would often recover ammonite fossils and carve snakes' heads onto the fossil to give credence to it!
See also: Fossils, Hilda, Jet

Authors

A number of authors, the first of whom was the poet Caedmon, have made their way to Whitby. Arguably the most well-known of them was Bram Stoker, who wrote the most famous vampire story of all time: *Dracula*. At around the time Stoker visited the town, Charles Dickens, Wilkie Collins, Lewis Carroll and Elizabeth Gaskell also arrived.

More recently a few supernatural stories have been written by authors using Whitby as the setting for their tales. Whether this is inspired by *Dracula*, or merely captures the mysterious atmosphere of the town, especially on a dark night when a sea fog rolls in, only the authors will know, but you might be tempted to read G. P. Taylor's *Shadowmancer* or *The Whitby Witches* by Robin Jarvis, which draws on some of the local legends of the town.

If the supernatural isn't for you, you may wish to try *Death's Disciple*, *The Eve of Murder*, *Bidding to Die*, and *Better the Devil you Know*, a series of crime novels set in Whitby and written by the cartoonist James Whitworth. Or, perhaps, you might enjoy the historical romance *Possession* by A. S. Byatt, which was also set in Whitby. The 2002 film of the book was also filmed in Whitby.

B

Bagdale Hall

If you follow Bagdale towards the train station, past the bottom of Pannett Park, you will discover, at the end of a row of three-storey town houses, an old Tudor manor house. This is Bagdale Hall, which dates back to 1516. It is one of the oldest habitable buildings in Whitby, though today it is a very agreeable hotel.

The hall was originally built for the Conyers family. George Conyers sold it to Whitby merchant Robert Bushell, whose grandson, Captain Browne Bushell, defended the castle for Parliament during the English Civil War. His cousin, Sir Hugh Cholmley, surrendered the castle to the Royalists, but Captain Bushell retook it, only to hand it back to Royalists. For this he paid with his life.

Given its history, Bagdale Hall is one of the most haunted houses in Whitby, boasting several ghosts and apparitions. One of the latter is a shapeless black mass which glides up and down the stairs. An old lady can be seen nursing a child outside room 2, and a ghostly figure of a man, in cape and hat, kisses lady guests on the cheek before disappearing through the wall.

It has been suggested that the latter may be Captain Bushell saying his goodbyes to his wife before his execution.

See also: Ghosts

Bede, The Venerable, or Saint Bede

It is from Bede that we find out about much of Whitby's early history. Bede, otherwise known as the Venerable or Saint Bede, was born in *c.* 673 and lived until 735. He was the foremost scholar of Anglo-Saxon England, if not Europe, being a poet, a theologian, a musician and a scientist, but he is most well-known for his book *Historia Ecclesiastica Gentis Anglorum* or The *Ecclesiastical History of the English People*, which was completed in 731.

Bede lived at the midpoint of the Dark Ages, the time from when the Romans left Britain, in *c.* AD 410, to the eleventh century, when William the Conqueror defeated King Harold II at Hastings.

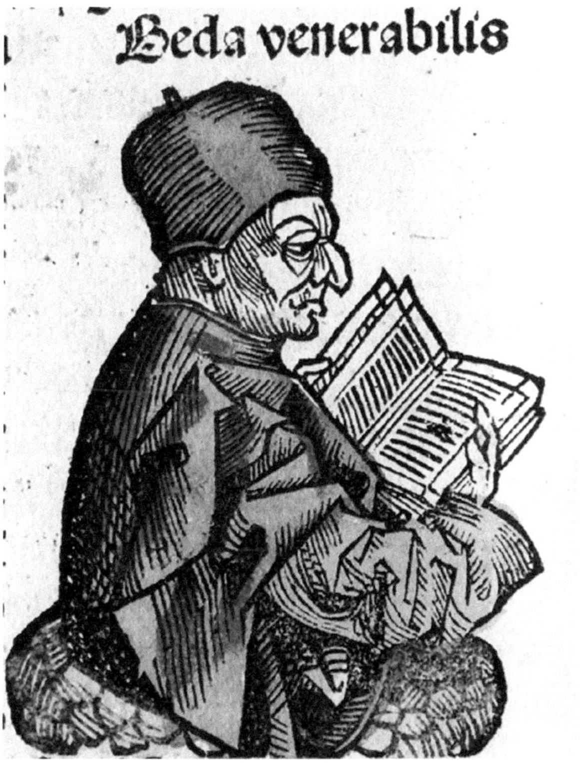

The Venerable Bede who chronicled much of the abbey's business, including the famous Synod of Whitby.

At the age of seven, Bede was granted an oblate at the newly established abbey of Wearmouth, now Monkwearmouth, which is part of Sunderland. In 682 he was transferred to Jarrow, where, apart from brief visits to York and Lindisfarne, he spent the rest of his life.

At the time, these two monasteries held the greatest libraries in England, and the books Bede found there were important in his writings, many of which survive. With regard to Whitby, Bede tells us how the settlement of his day obtained its name. He gives us an account of the Synod of Whitby, of the life of Saint Hilda and of Caedmon, who, in later life, became a member of the religious community at Whitby.

Bede's *History* is the most important source for our understanding of early England. (Bede's Feast Day is 25, formerly 27, May).

Brewing

Whitby has a long history of brewing, something which should not be unexpected when one considers that the town was created around the original seventh-century abbey, where the brewing of beer would have been an essential occupation for the monks. After the abbey was refounded in the eleventh century, this would have continued to be the case. The development of the town as a port, together with fishing, whaling and shipbuilding, would have created a market for beer, which, as elsewhere in the country, was, at first, supplied by small brewers working from their homes, some of which were converted into inns and public houses.

It was not until the nineteenth century that sizeable brewing firms were set up in Whitby. Two of the earliest were Corner & Readman, of the Marine Parade Brewery, and Robert Raine of the Esk Brewery. The latter brewery has a complicated history. It was occupied by Clarkson & Weighill and, after that, by John Weighill & Sons. The firms at the Marine Parade and Esk breweries collectively became known as Whitby Breweries. They were acquired by the combined Scarborough Breweries: The Scarborough Brewing Co. and the Old Brewery, Scarborough. This took place in 1897 when a firm constructed out the four firms – two in Scarborough, two in Whitby – became known as the Scarborough & Whitby Breweries Ltd (SWBL).

The premises of the two Whitby breweries did not survive the merger, leaving the town without its own brewery for some time. The firm of John L. Hunt Ltd, of York, acquired an interest in SWBL and took a controlling interest in the firm in 1913. Hunt's was taken over by J. W. Cameron & Co. of the Lion Brewery, West Hartlepool, in 1953, the brewery in Scarborough closing a year later. Since then, Cameron's have been the subject of a takeover and were once in the hands of the Wolverhampton & Dudley Breweries who sold Cameron's, and their subsidiaries, to the Castle Eden Brewery in 2002. However, the Cameron name has been retained and, in that name, something of Whitby's old brewery history is retained.

In recent years, a number of microbreweries have been established in Whitby. They include the Whitby's Own Brewery, at the Old Workhouse at Whitby in 1988, though, in 1992, it moved to larger premises at The Ropery. Unfortunately, brewing ceased in 1997 after a failed attempt to acquire a public house to provide a regular outlet. The premises were taken over in the same year by the Black Dog Brewery, which had clear Dracula connections, but production stopped in 2000. In 2013, the Whitby Brewery was established. It remains in business on the East Cliff, near Whitby Abbey.

Bridge (Swing)

You cannot get from one side of Whitby to the other without crossing over a bridge and there is no bridge more prominent than the swing bridge that crosses the River Esk. Before this bridge was erected there were many other bridges that spanned the river.

The first mention of a bridge in Whitby dates to 1351 when King Edward III allowed tolls to be collected for the purpose of maintaining a bridge over the River Esk. Just over 200 years later, the tolls collected totalled around £6 per year, which showed how important the bridge was to people.

In 1407, local man John Schilbotyll left an oak tree in his will to be used for repairs to the Whitby bridge! There are few details of that bridge but it can be assumed that it was made of wood as a 1629 agreement mentions replacing the wooden bridge

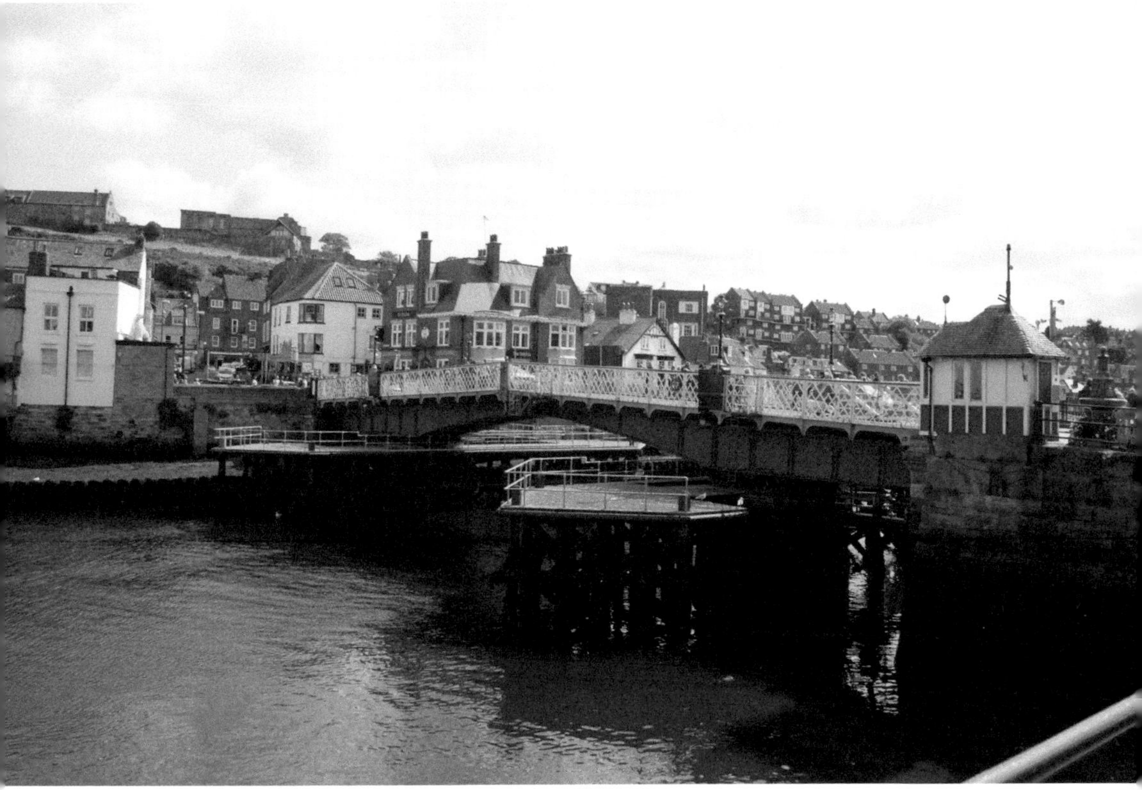

The iconic swing bridge across the River Esk. This bridge links the east and west sides of Whitby. There have been many different types of bridge here.

with one with moving parts to allow shipping traffic to reach further up the Esk. That bridge would have had ropes, blocks, and pulleys to assist the moving parts.

This new bridge was in use until 1766 when it was replaced with a drawbridge designed to lift and allow the passage of shipping. However, the rigging of these ships would often become caught in the bridge's mechanisms. By the 1830s the bridge was in a poor state of repair and the shipyards of Whitby were building bigger ships.

The bridge needed to be replaced once more and in 1832 a wooden bridge was ordered that would open horizontally, the planes swinging open to allow ships to pass and reduce the risk of entanglement. The swing bridge proved highly popular, appearing in photographs of that era. It was opened by hand-operated winches and later by water-powered engines. But, sadly, the shipping industry was building bigger ships and the bridge wouldn't open wide enough.

In 1906 a steel swing bridge was designed and constructed, which was designed to open wider. It used electric motors and was built by the engineers Heenan and Froude of Manchester, who had also built the Blackpool Tower. The current bridge has now stood for longer than any of its predecessors.

See also: Shipbuilding

C

Caedmon

There once lived, at Whitby Abbey, a lay brother who cared for the animals. His name was Caedmon. He was no musician but, one night, he was asked to join in with the partying monks. However, knowing no songs, he went to the stables to go to sleep. That night he dreamt that a person came to visit him and asked him to sing about 'the beginning of created things'. At first Caedmon refused but then began to recite a

A stunning view of Caedmon's Cross in St Mary's churchyard. (Picture courtesy of Aubrey Jacobs-Tyson)

poem that praised God. Upon awakening, Caedmon went to see the Abbess (possibly Saint Hilda) and told her of his dream. She believed that Caedmon had had divine inspiration and commissioned him to write a poem based on some part of sacred doctrine, probably to test him.

When he returned, the Abbess was so impressed that Caedmon was invited to take holy orders and become a monk. Caedmon was taught by the other monks in all matters relating to holy scripture and Caedmon would often turn these into verse. Caedmon lived as a monk until sometime between 679 and 684, when he had a premonition of his death. He lodged in the abbey's hospice, dying after receiving the Holy Eucharist.

In 1898 a cross was erected in the churchyard of St Mary's Church dedicated to Caedmon. The intricate stone carvings depict Caedmon and an inscription on the base of the cross reads, 'To the glory of God and in memory of Caedmon the father of English sacred song. Fell asleep hard by, 680.' This cross still stands today and is a focal point at the top of the 199 Steps.

See also: Graveyard, Hilda

Carroll, Lewis

A Victorian novelist who knew Whitby quite well (he stayed at No. 5 East Terrace in the town on at least seven occasions) was Lewis Carroll, otherwise Charles Lutwidge Dodgson. He was an Oxford mathematician but remains famous as the author of *Alice's Adventures in Wonderland* and *Through the Looking Glass.*

It is often not appreciated that Lewis Carroll's first publication was in Whitby. This was a satirical poem entitled 'The Lady of the Ladle', which was published in the *Whitby Gazette* during Carroll's visit of 1854.

There is an account of Carroll's stay at Whitby by one of his companions (a group made up of fellow mathematicians). Dr Thomas Fowler recalled that Carroll used to sit on a rock on the beach, telling stories to a circle of eager young listeners of both boys and girls. Fowler believed that this was how, as he put it, 'Alice was incubated', but it is known that Carroll's later writing had deep personal origins.

Whitby was probably important to him in several different ways. The poem the 'Walrus and the Carpenter' is often thought to have been the product of Carroll's visits to Whitby but, when he was there, in 1854, it is likely that he was experimenting with how stories might be told, particularly to children. He used the direct approach when at the beach but, at the same time, he was establishing himself as humorous journalist in the pages of the local newspaper. The 'Walrus and the Carpenter' did not appear until the publication of *Through the Looking Glass* in 1871.

See also: Authors

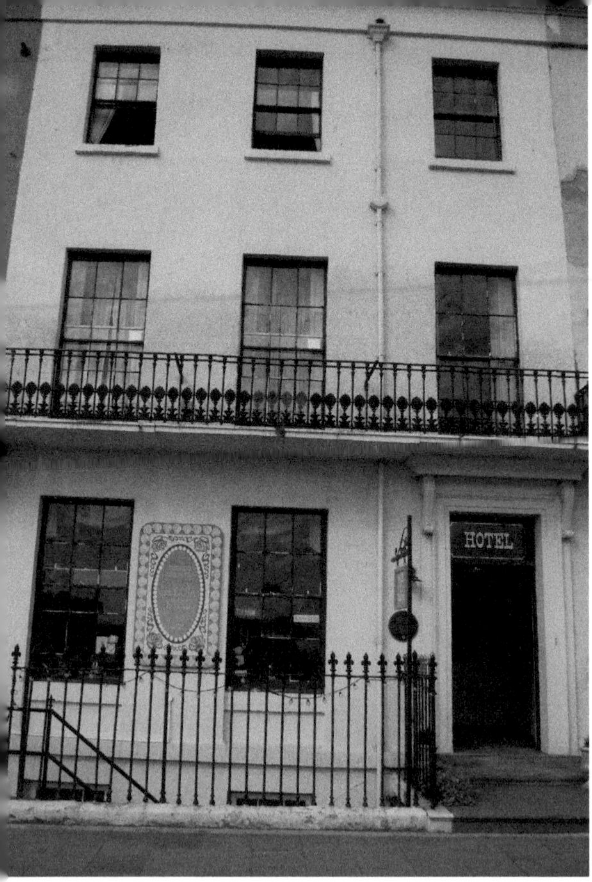

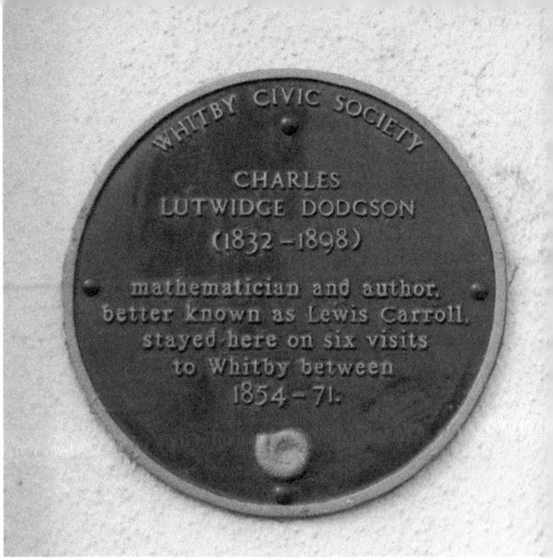

Above: A plaque commemorating Lewis Carroll. Some of his early work was published in the *Whitby Gazette*.

Left: Lewis Carroll, the creator of *Alice in Wonderland*, stayed here in the mid-1800s.

Cholmley, Sir Richard

In 1539, at the dissolution of Whitby Abbey, Richard Cholmley obtained a lease of the abbey site and some of the property that had been part of the abbey. At the time of Edward VI, the property was sold, without Cholmley's agreement, by the Crown to John, Earl of Warwick, and again, in 1551, the abbey buildings were sold on to Sir Edward Yorke, from whom the property was purchased by Sir Richard Cholmley, who had, by this time, been knighted.

It was Sir Richard who commenced the Cholmley association with the abbey and particularly with Whitby Hall, which was built on the site of the Abbot's House in 1580. Sir Richard was a descendent of the Cholmondeley's of Cheshire who had resided in that county from the time of the Conquest.

See also: Whitby Hall

Coat of Arms

Whitby's coat of arms has been updated on several occasions but the most well-known is a shield with three ammonites (or serpents) on a blue background representative of the sea. The shield is surmounted by a mitre, which was usually described as a bishop's mitre, but it might equally be a mitre worn by an abbot. There is a banner or motto which reads FUIMUS ET SUMUS, which translates as 'We have been, and we are', establishing the continuity of the place.

Collins, Wilkie

Charles Dickens was responsible for encouraging his contemporary Wilkie Collins to visit Whitby. Collins, who was also a novelist, rivalled Dickens for popularity, though the two men were friends and they worked together on several projects.

Collins was in Whitby in 1861 when he was accompanied by Caroline Graves, who is thought to have been the inspiration for his novel *The Woman in White*, which had been published the year before. They had probably met in 1856 and two years later, they were living together, something which lasted, almost continuously, until Collins died in 1889.

The reference to Caroline being the inspiration for *The Woman in White* comes not from Collins himself, but the son of the artist Sir John Everett Millais. In a biography of his father, he describes a melodramatic night-time meeting of Millais, Wilkie Collins and Charles Collins with a distraught woman running away from a man who is keeping her prisoner under mesmeric influence. There is a scene in *The Woman in White* which is reminiscent of this incident.

See also: Authors

Cook, Captain James

Captain James Cook is possibly one of the most important sailors and explorers of all time, having explored Hawaii and Australia. Although not a Whitby man by birth (he was born up the road in Marton), he moved to Staithes when he was sixteen years old to work in a haberdashery shop.

After eighteen months the lure of the sea was so great that Cook moved to Whitby and into lodgings on Grape Lane. These can be visited today as it is the site of the Captain Cook museum.

Cook excelled in his new seafaring career and was soon promoted following his apprenticeship, but he realised that, to go further in life, he would need to join the Royal Navy. He signed up prior to the Seven Years' War and, after serving in North America, Cook showed his talent for exploration, navigation and cartography by drafting maps of the St Lawrence River and the coast of Newfoundland. This seems to have sparked his desire for exploration as he said that he intended to go 'farther than any man has been before me, but as far as I think it is possible for a man to go'.

In 1768, Cook got his chance and was promoted to lieutenant in order to command a joint Royal Society and Royal Navy expedition to witness the Transit of Venus (an astronomical event where Venus would pass before the sun) in 1769. He was also to discover the mysterious Terra Australis Incognito (the Unknown Land of the South), which had been rumoured to exist since Roman times and had been accidentally 'discovered' or visited several times through the centuries – although no one had ever properly explored it.

In August 1768, cook set sail from Plymouth in the ship HMS *Endeavour* and, after achieving his first objective (the Transit of Venus), he continued his mission, which was to sail south to search for the unknown continent, then turn west to New Zealand, where he and his crew were the second group of Europeans to visit the land.

Cook was to map the islands of New Zealand and finally choose his own route home. There was no explicit mention of Australia, yet Cook managed to navigate the

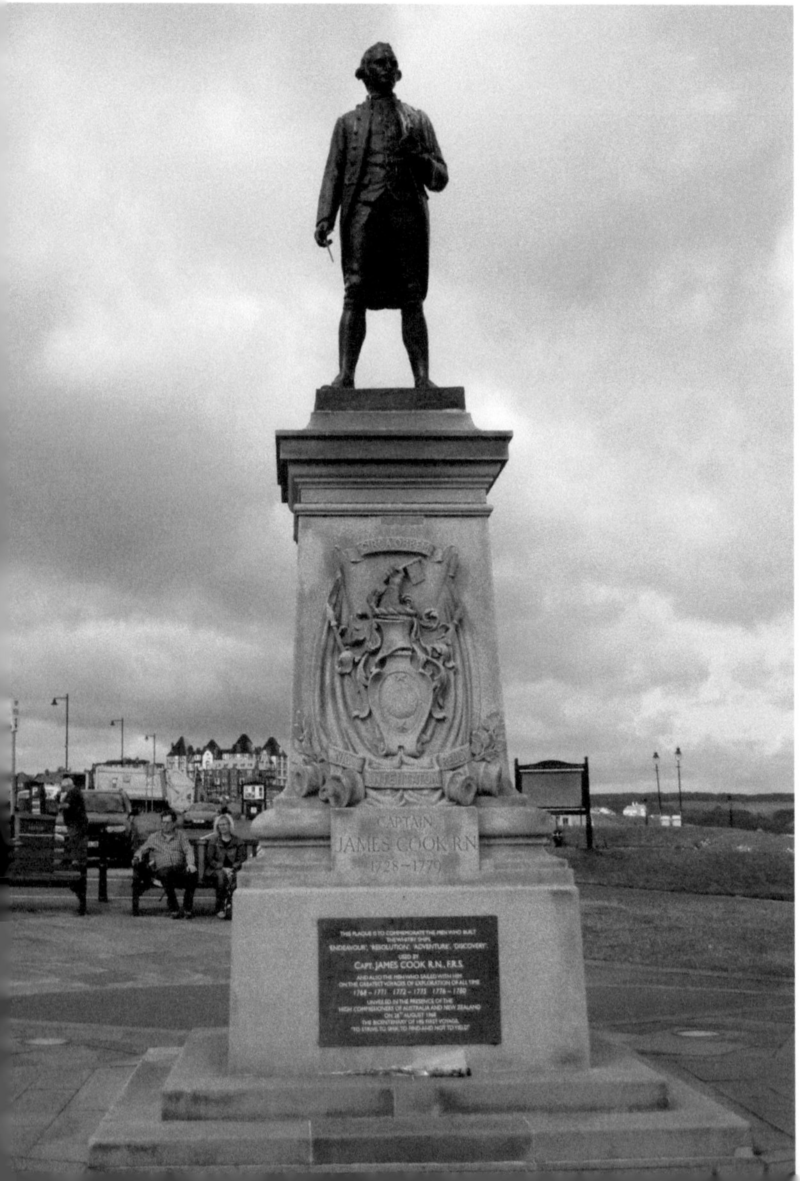

The statue of Captain Cook stands on the edge of the West Cliff – all four of his ships were built in Whitby.

Endeavour in such a way that on 17 April 1770, the east coast of Australia was sighted. Cook intended to navigate northwards and, in doing so, landed at a bay that would later be known as Botany Bay. On 6 May 1770, Cook sailed on and sailed past an inlet they named as Port Jackson, which would later become Sydney when it was settled by the First Fleet, who set up a penal colony there.

Cook went on to claim the eastern coast of Australia, naming it New South Wales, before returning to England. He would later command two more voyages of discovery in HMS *Resolution*. On the third mission, the *Resolution* was joined by HMS *Discovery*. Interestingly, the *Endeavour*, *Resolution*, and *Discovery* were all built in Whitby and later commandeered by the Royal Navy. On his third voyage, Cook fell into a dispute with the Hawaiians at Kealakekua Bay and was killed whilst trying to kidnap the King of Hawaii.

Captain Cook's legacy lives on in Whitby and evidence of his ties to the town are all around. On the West Cliff, near the Whalebone Arch, you will find a large statue commemorating him. The Captain Cook Museum is in Grape Lane. If you visit Pannett Park you will also find the South Seas Garden and the Whitby Museum also holds several artefacts from Cook's voyages of discovery. These include a copy of his probate will, a report on the Transit of Venus, and a hand-drawn map made by Cook himself when he surveyed the coast of Newfoundland.

See also: *Endeavour*, *Resolution*, Shipbuilding

Crow's Nest

You may wonder what that barrel fastened to the top of an old ship's mast has to do with Whitby. This position, at the highest point of the ship, was so effective that it remained the most important form of early warning for shipping until the invention of radar in the early twentieth century.

The name Crow's Nest is allegedly derived from an ancient practice used by Vikings to navigate to the nearest land. They would release ravens and crows (from a cage kept at the top of the mast) and would watch the direction in which the birds flew because they would take the most direct route to land.

The first Crow's Nest looked like a barrel lashed to a mast when it was invented in 1807, by William Scoresby, Senior, an Arctic seafarer who made his fortune hunting whales. He wanted to provide a place of shelter for a ship's navigator, possibly following his 1806 expedition where he took his ship further north than any other ship had travelled before, and the barrel was the solution he devised.

If you haven't already guessed, William Scoresby Senior was from Whitby and today his grave can be found in the churchyard of St Mary's Church overlooking the harbour that brought him so much fame and fortune. A replica of the barrel-type Crow's Nest can be found in the Whitby Museum.

See also: Whaling; Scoresby, William (Senior)

D

Dickens, Charles

Charles Dickens stayed in Whitby at Mulgrave Castle, which is a few miles out of the town. The castle, as it was in Dickens's time, is the home of the Marquess of Normanby, whom Dickens counted among his friends. Dickens dedicated his novel *Dombey and Son*, which was published in monthly parts between 1846 and 1848, to the marchioness. In the story, the sombreness of the Dombey mansion is contrasted with the warm-heartedness, if not very business-like environment, of the shop of Solomon Gills. It is a device that Dickens used to effect in other novels. Of these, *A Christmas Carol*, published in 1843, is the best known and, in this instance, Scrooge's miserable counting house is contrasted with the poverty and simple pleasures of the home of the Cratchit family.

There is a connection between these two novels. Although Dickens had visited Whitby as early as 1836, when its famous railway was still under construction, he made the journey to North Yorkshire again, in 1844, when he attended the funeral of another friend, Charles Smithson, a lawyer with a practice in Malton, not far from Whitby.

Dickens had visited the firm's offices in Malton's Chancery Lane on a previous occasion. It is credited as being the inspiration for Scrooge's counting house in

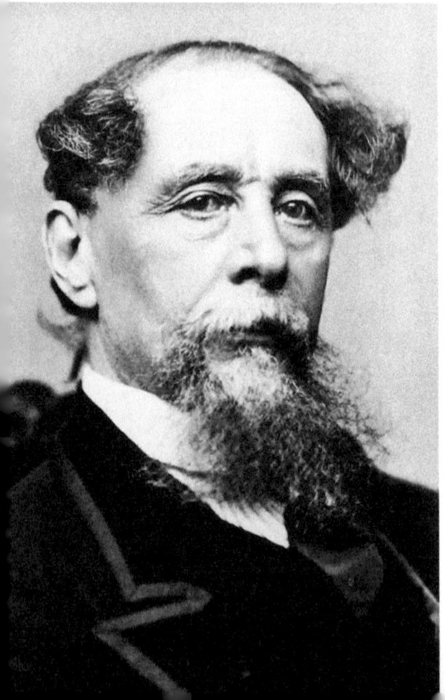

Charles Dickens was a frequent visitor to Whitby, staying at the nearby Musgrave Castle.

A Christmas Carol, the character of Scrooge himself emerging from the office as visited by Dickens. Mr Smithson's house was Easthope Hall, near Malton, and, when Dickens was there, he met the lady on whom Mrs Sarah Gamp is based. She is the alcoholic midwife and nurse in the novel *Martin Chuzzlewit*.

After the funeral at Malton, Dickens travelled to Lythe, where Mulgrave Castle stands. Lord Normanby agreed to show Dickens the countryside around Whitby and they are reputed to have enjoyed a meal at the White Horse & Griffin, in Church Street in the town. Dickens also persuaded his friend and fellow author Wilkie Collins to visit Whitby.

See also: Authors, Mulgrave Castle

Discovery

Discovery was the consort ship of James Cook's third and final voyage to the Pacific Ocean, in 1776–80. The ship was a collier, built by Longbourne's in 1774. It was of 299 tons and, in 1775, the vessel, then known as *Diligence*, was purchased by the Royal Navy. Cook had extensive alterations undertaken.

Discovery was commanded by Charles Clerke, who had sailed on Cook's previous two expeditions, but when Cook was killed in Hawaii, Clerke transferred to HMS *Resolution* and John Gore took command of *Discovery*.

The ship returned to England in 1780 and was converted into a transport vessel based at Woolwich. In 1781, *Discovery* became a dockyard craft, still at Woolwich, but it was broken up at Chatham in 1797.

See also: Cook, Captain James; *Endeavour*; *Resolution*; Shipbuilding

Dracula

You cannot come to Whitby and not notice that there is a certain vampire associated with the town. Published in 1897, the novel *Dracula* has never been out of print and has been made into, or inspired, over 215 films. However, if your only experience of Dracula has been in film, you will probably not know why Dracula and Whitby are linked. If you read the novel you soon see why.

Having landed at Whitby, Dracula sought refuge in the grave of a suicide in St Mary's churchyard. The gravestone was the favourite seat of two young holidaymakers, Lucy Westenra and Mina Murray. Lucy is later attacked by Dracula and transformed into a vampire. Mina is also attacked but is saved from turning into the Undead by Professor Van Helsing.

Whitby has embraced its connections with Dracula and today tourists can visit The Dracula Experience – an immersive adventure through the tale of Dracula. Guided ghost walks recount some of the local legends that inspired the Dracula story and

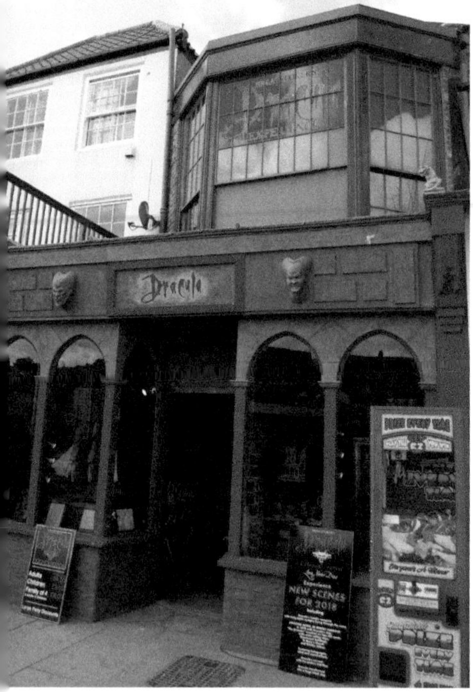

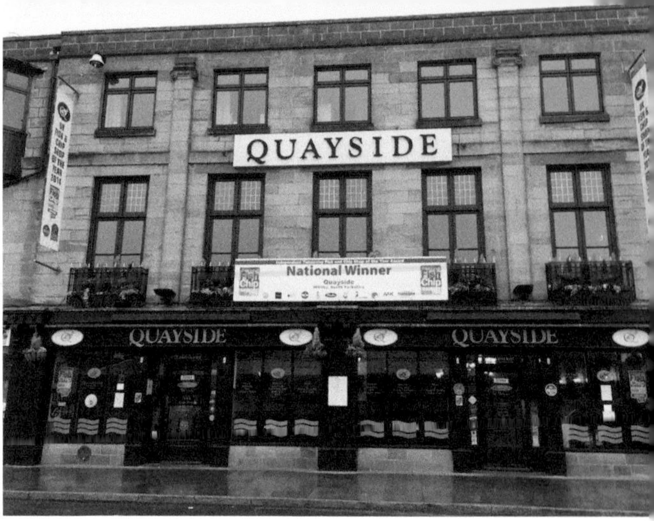

Above: The Quayside restaurant was once the Whitby Public Lending Library where Bram Stoker read about the real Dracula, a Transylvanian warlord. Stoker used his name for his vampire count.

Left: The Dracula Experience on Marine Parade. This tells the story of Dracula to those brave enough to enter.

hundreds of tourists will climb to the top of the 199 Steps in search of Dracula's grave. The novel has also inspired the Goths to use Whitby as its base for the biannual Whitby Goth Weekend. For more, see this author's own book *Dracula's Whitby* (Amberley Publishing).

See also: Authors; Ghosts; Stoker, Bram

St Mary's Church featured heavily in *Dracula*. Here Dracula rested in the grave of a suicide. Mind where you step!

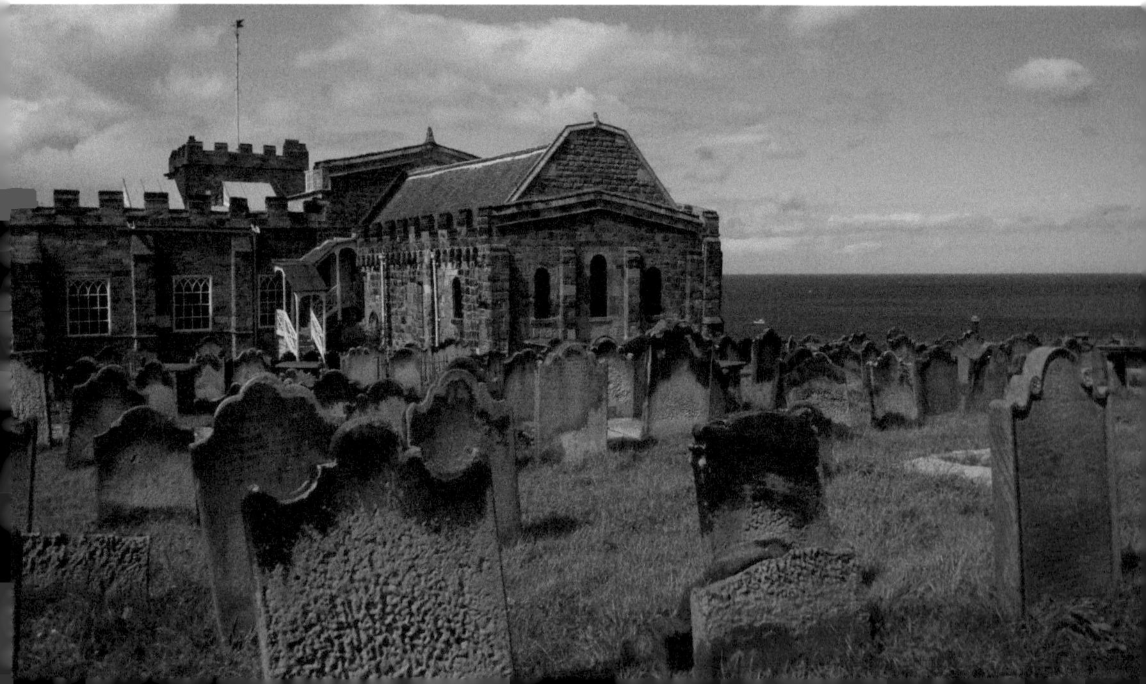

E

Easter

Easter is unlike Christmas as it never falls on the same date each year. The date of Easter is worked out based on a lunisolar calendar that has a 532-year cycle. However, this wasn't always the case as, in the kingdom of Northumbria (where Whitby was located), two methods were used to calculate Easter and, as can be expected, it caused a bit of confusion, some feasting whilst others were still observing Lent.

There was the Ionian practice and the Roman practice, the first being the tradition of the Irish missionaries who converted much of the north of England to Christianity. The latter followed the customs of Rome.

In order to find a solution, King Oswy, of Northumbria, looked to religious leaders and a synod was held at Hilda's monastery. The 'Synod of Whitby' was to have long-lasting consequences for the Christian church. Some argued that the Ionian system should be adopted, Saint Hilda among them, as it was the practice of Columba – founder of the Ionian movement and a saint of great holiness. The counter argument was that the Roman position should be adopted as it was what was used in Rome where Saint Peter had lived, taught, suffered, and was buried. Since both sides recognised the unchallengeable authority of Saint Peter, they agreed to follow the Roman practice.

See also: Abbey, Hilda, Synod of Whitby

Endeavour

Whitby is, rightly, proud of its connections with this historic ship. Captain Cook was commissioned to conduct his explorations by the Royal Navy. They needed to provide him with a ship that would be best suited to the task.

Colliers, which carried coal from the north-east of England, were considered ideal as their strong construction and flat-bottomed hulls were able to navigate shallow water. The ships could be beached and re-floated, which made repairs and resupply so much easier where docks and piers did not exist.

All four of Captain Cook's ships were Whitby-built colliers, the most famous being the *Endeavour* and the *Resolution*. The other two, *Discovery* and *Adventure*, still played vital roles, the latter being the first ship to circumnavigate the globe from west to east.

The *Endeavour* was built in 1764 by the shipbuilder Thomas Fishburn and was named *The Earl of Pembroke* before being bought, for £2,840 10 shillings and 11 pence, by the Royal Navy for Cook's first mission in 1768. The refit required to make her suitable for her mission cost almost as much as the purchase price. The last change to be made was the name. *Endeavour* was already in use as a naval cutter, so the given name became *His Majesty's Bark the Endeavour*. Bark related to the type of ship that the *Endeavour* was with her three masts.

On her voyages she sailed up the eastern coast of Australia, landing at Botany Bay before continuing onward. The *Endeavour* ran aground on the Great Barrier Reef and, in order to sail off the reef, it needed to be substantially lightened, so the guns and other supplies totalling around 50 tons were thrown overboard, after which substantial repairs were carried out.

The *Endeavour* returned to England in July 1771, putting into Dover. It was quite an unexpected return, especially when there had been much speculation about whether the ship had been lost at sea. It was after the return that Captain Cook was about to embark on his next voyage of discovery but, alas, not with *Endeavour*. The ship was refitted as a naval transport and made three trips to the Falklands, the last trip being used to evacuate the Falkland Islanders in April 1774.

Later in 1774, *Endeavour* was decommissioned and sold for £645 to Mather & Co., a large shipping corporation. During the American War of Independence, Mather & Co. offered the *Endeavour* as a transport ship, but it was rejected as unfit for service. They tried again, changing its name to *Lord Sandwich*, but it was recognised and rejected again. A third attempt, under the imaginative name of *Lord Sandwich 2*, was successful.

Endeavour set sail for the Americas where she served for a short time as a prison ship before taking part in the attack of Newport in August 1778. In order to prevent the French Fleet (who were allied to the Americans) from entering the harbour, the

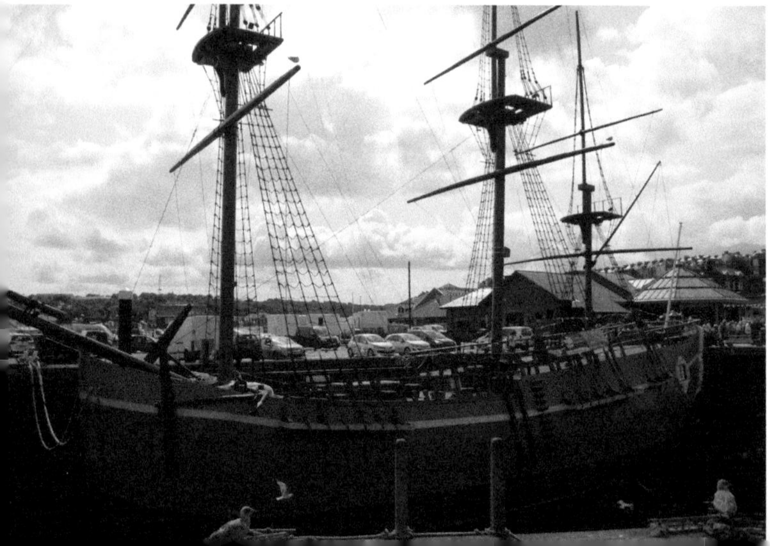

Captain Cook's most famous ship, the *Endeavour*, was built as a collier in Whitby. This replica is now moored in Whitby harbour.

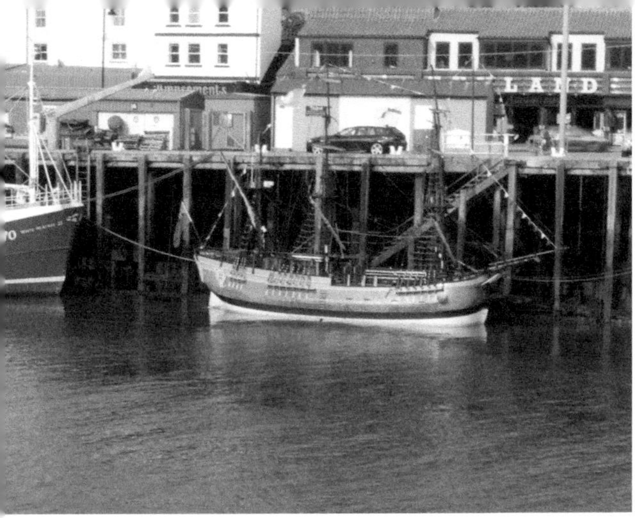

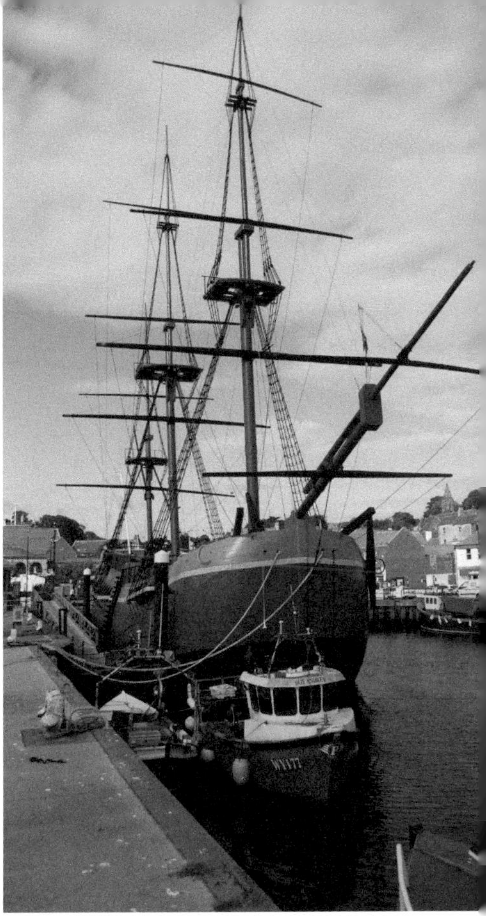

Above: Whitby is home to two *Endeavour* replicas. This one is somewhat smaller and takes tourists on short trips from the harbour.

Right: The *Endeavour* replica has sailed around the world, following Captain Cook's adventures.

British Commander ordered several vessels to be scuttled and sunk. On 4 August 1778, *Endeavour* was lost to the sea.

Today the wreck has yet to be definitively identified, although there are strong indications that *Endeavour* has been found. Its cannons were recovered from the Great Barrier Reef in 1969, and in 1994 a replica of *Endeavour* was built in Australia and visited Whitby in 1997 and 2002 before returning to Australia as a museum ship. In Whitby you are lucky enough to see two replicas of *Endeavour*. One is around half-size and provides regular trips down the coast, and the other is a museum ship, which was the second full-sized replica built. This is now moored in Whitby harbour.

See also: Cook, Captain James; *Discovery*; *Resolution*; Shipbuilding

Esk

You cannot fail to notice that the River Esk cuts through the very centre of Whitby, leading out to the sea. On one side of the swing bridge is the marina where hundreds of boats are moored, and on the other, the quayside and the piers.

The 28-mile-long river is the only east-flowing river in Yorkshire that empties directly into the North Sea. All other rivers either find their way into the Tees or the Humber Estuary.

The importance of the Esk can be found in its name, which is derived from the Celtic word *Isca*, which means water or stream, indicating that this was the most significant river in the area. The river has retained its importance, being the home of fishing and whaling fleets and a successful shipbuilding industry.

The Esk has salmon and sea trout and is the only Yorkshire river where endangered freshwater pearl mussel can be found. The river starts in the North York Moors where three small becks come together to create the Esk. It meanders through Eskdale, passing through many villages along the way, including Lealholme, which was once famous for its Victorian rockery gardens at Crunkly Ghyll. Sadly, these have been washed away following many of the Esk's bouts of flooding.

As the river reaches Whitby a curious tradition known as the Planting of the Penny Hedge takes place. The tradition recreates an act of forgiveness for a callous murder

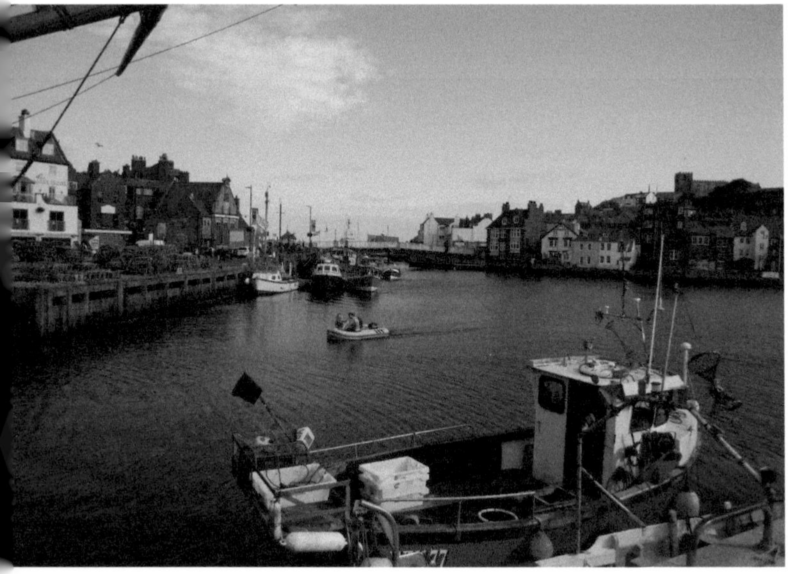

The Esk flows through Whitby to the North Sea. The Esk is both a place of work and a place for leisure for many.

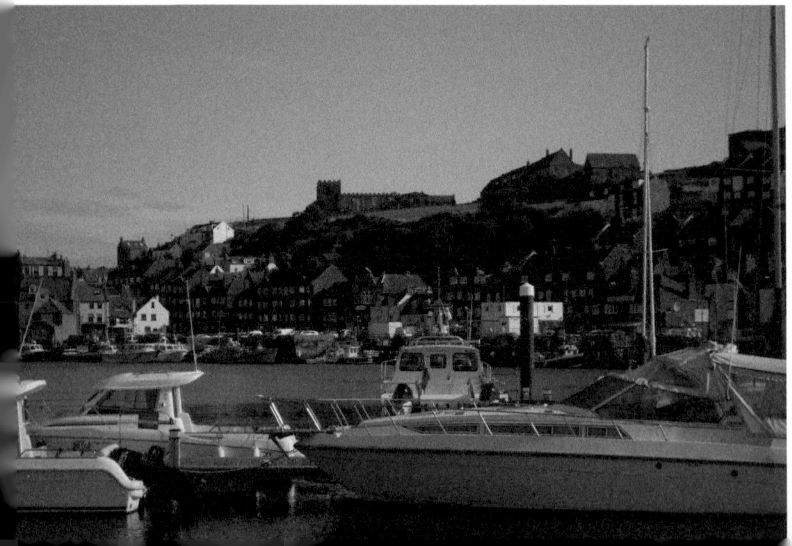

Whitby Marina is home to both working boats and pleasure boats.

in the twelfth century. Sea fishing trips, pleasure boat rides, and the annual regatta all take place in Whitby.

As rivers go, the Esk is quite interesting and if you feel inclined to get to know the river, you may want to trek along the Esk Valley Walk, a long-distance footpath which starts at the source on the North York Moors, passes through Castleton, Lealholme, Grosmont and finishes at Whitby. It is waymarked by a leaping salmon sign and can take up to four days to complete, or you may wish to follow some of the shorter, day-long sections.

See also: Fishing, Penny Hedge, Regatta, Shipbuilding, Whaling

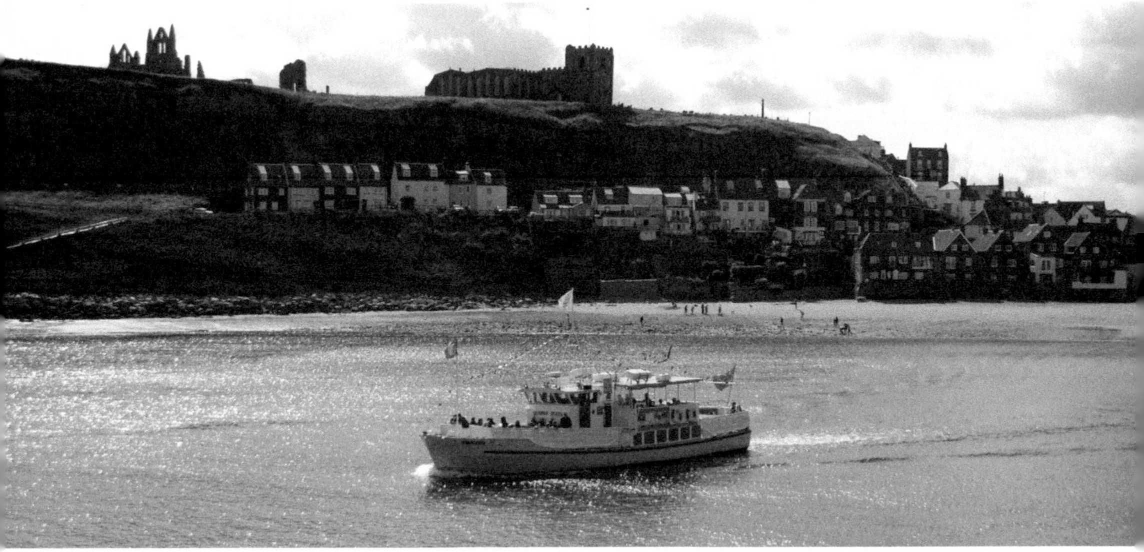

Above: One of the many tour boats that operate on the River Esk.

Below: The Esk has remained an important part of Whitby life. The boats have changed but the views remain the same.

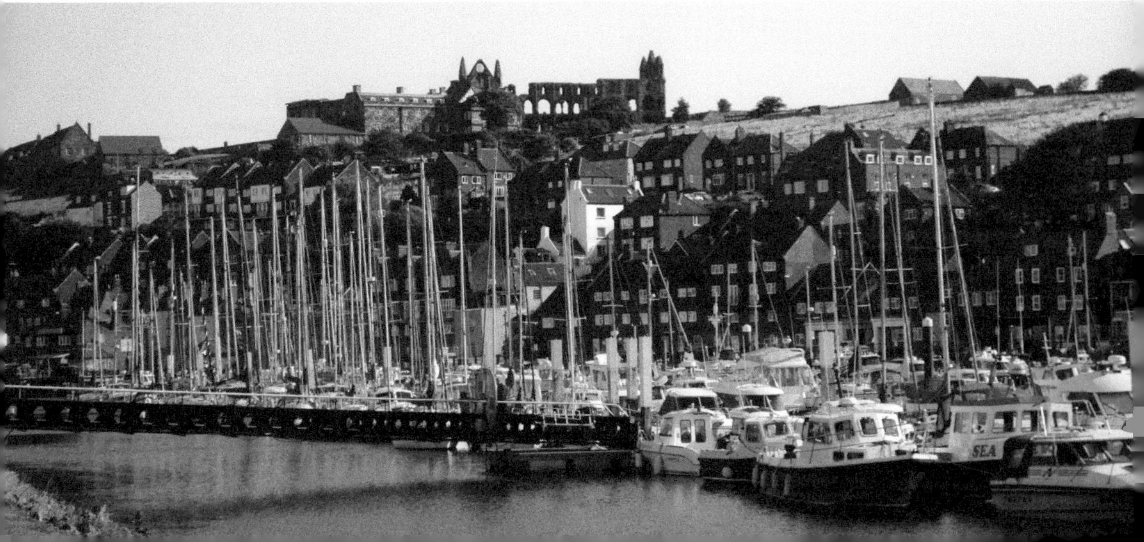

F

Fishing

Whitby is, first and foremost, a fishing town. There is no escaping that when you visit. From the marina you will see trawlers, day boats, and chartered fishing vessels moored up or making their way to and from the fishing grounds that they rely on for their livelihood.

Whitby produces delicious smoked herrings, or kippers, smoked on Henrietta Street, in town, and found on the breakfast menus of many Whitby guest houses. Similarly, there appear to be countless fish and chip shops and restaurants in the town. In fact, Whitby is synonymous with many things: Dracula, Captain Cook, the abbey, and its fish and chips!

The fish and chip shops that you will find in Whitby are feted by the famous. Celebrity chef Rick Stein has described the Magpie Café as the best fish and chip restaurant in the land. The Magpie is easy to spot as there is always a queue of people waiting for a seat stretching along the quayside. Speaking of Quayside, the fish and chip restaurant of the same name is also a multiple-award winner and boasts the accolade of being the site of the old Whitby Public Lending Library where Bram Stoker first learned about the real-life Dracula.

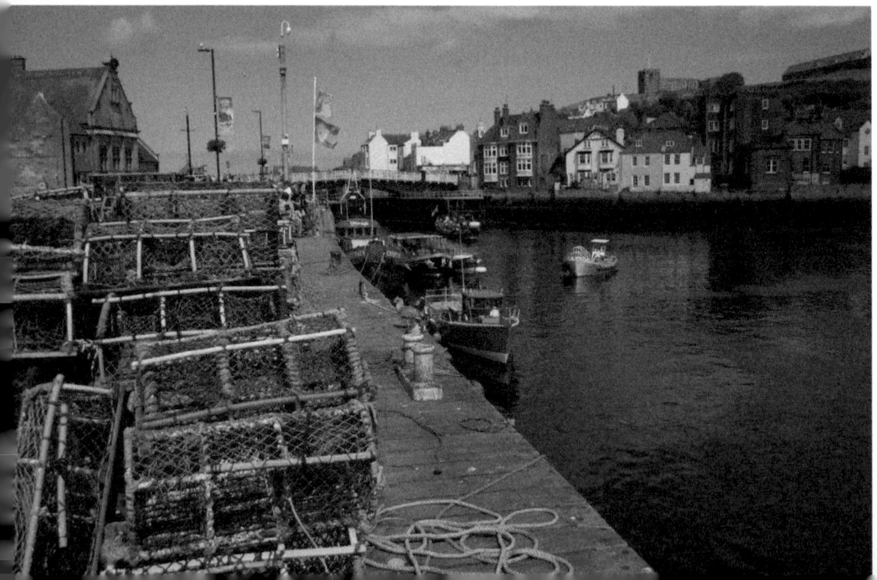

Piles of lobster pots and fishing boats moored along the harbour leave you in no doubt that Whitby remains a working fishing port.

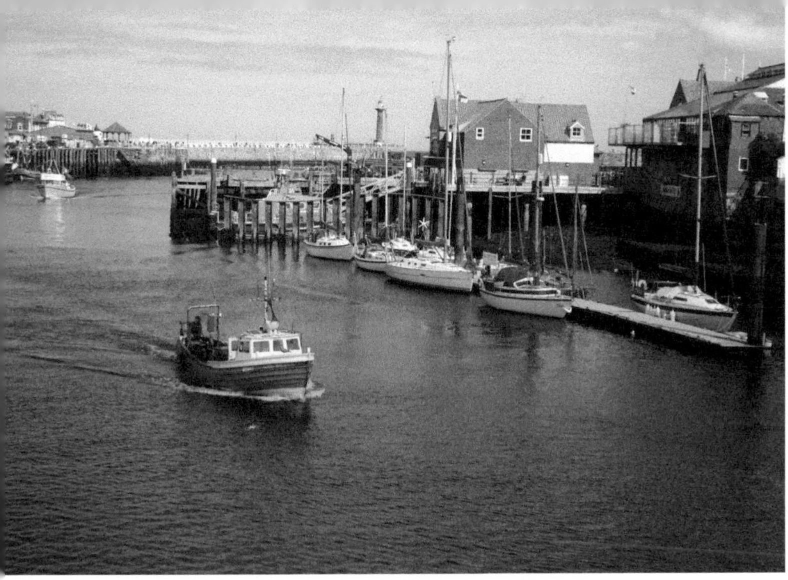

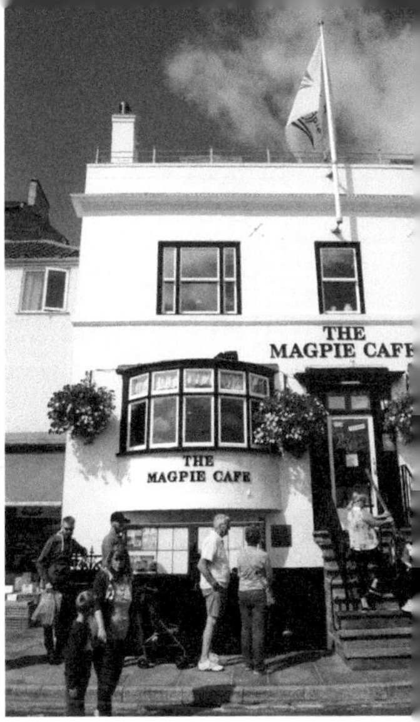

Above left: A small fishing boat returns to harbour with its catch. Fishing remains one of Whitby's biggest industries.

Above right: The famous Magpie Café. People queue for a table and to enjoy some of the best fish and chips in the country.

It is always a pleasure to watch the trawlers come in and land their catch and see the boxes of freshly iced fish stacked up in the small fish market. In days gone by this would have been the epicentre of business in Whitby. In the 1930s, big game fishing for bluefin tuna was popular in the waters off Whitby and neighbouring Scarborough. This was until the stocks declined in the 1950s, and the tuna became locally extinct due to herring and mackerel fishing.

The bluefin tuna is arguably one of the strongest fish in the world and there were tales of monumental battles between fishermen, armed with powerful rods, and the huge tuna. The British record for catching the biggest tuna occurred in the waters off Whitby in 1933, when Lorenzo Mitchell-Henry landed a tuna weighing 851 pounds (386 kg). The women's British record was achieved in the same waters in 1947, by Dr Bidi Evans who landed a tuna weighing 714 pounds (324kg).

See also: Kippers, Scampi, Whitby Whale

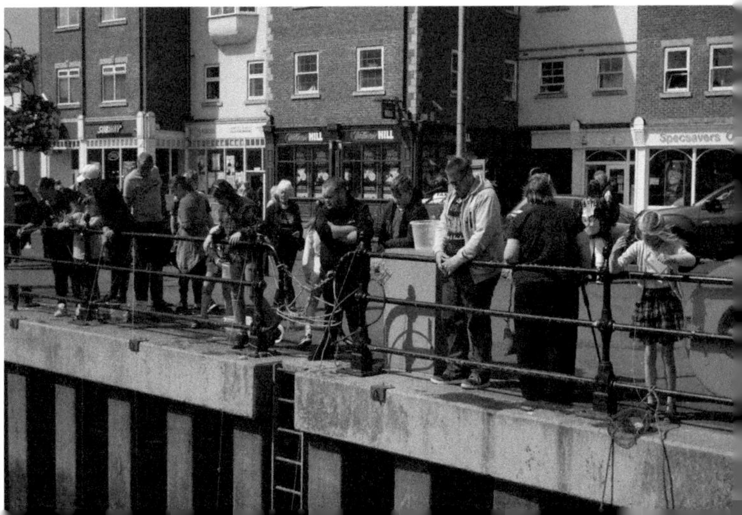

A popular Whitby pastime is 'crabbing'. Tourists and locals try to catch crabs from the harbourside.

Fossils

Whitby is geologically renowned for its great fossil finds and is an excellent place for anyone to come and search for fossils. Whilst hunting for fossils is not inherently dangerous, the locations where the fossils may be found in Whitby are. Most of the fossils are revealed because of the deterioration of the cliffs where rockfall is a constant danger. Similarly, the slippery rocks of the shoreline, and the threat of the incoming tide, are significant. If sensible precautions are made, a great deal of fun can be had.

Whitby is rich in fossils and many have been discovered. Of these the ammonite fossils have been collected in abundance. They had been thought to have been petrified snakes, turned to stone by Hilda, but fossils of plants and large marine reptiles were also discovered.

One of the earliest fossil discoveries in the Whitby area occurred when alum was being mined in 1758 and the skeleton of a prehistoric crocodile was extracted by Captain William Chapman. Teleosaurus chapmani, as it came to be known, was later donated to the British Museum.

More recently a 15-kg fossil of a dinosaur vertebrae was discovered at Whitby by an amateur fossil hunter named Alan Gurr. It was believed to by 176 million years old and is thought to come from a long-necked, long-tailed sauropod like a brontosaurus. Even today it is possible to see fossilised footprints of dinosaurs in the rocks below the cliffs.

Fossils became big business in Whitby and quarrymen would sell their finds to make money. The Revd George Young helped found the Whitby Literary and Philosophical Society in order to preserve some of these fossils and the society later became the Whitby Museum. Today you can see many examples of fossils found at Whitby at the museum, and you can also buy some examples at many shops in Whitby. Or, if you are feeling adventurous, pick up a guidebook and go for a search yourself, remembering to take the right safety precautions before you do.

See also: Ammonites, Hilda, Jet, Museum

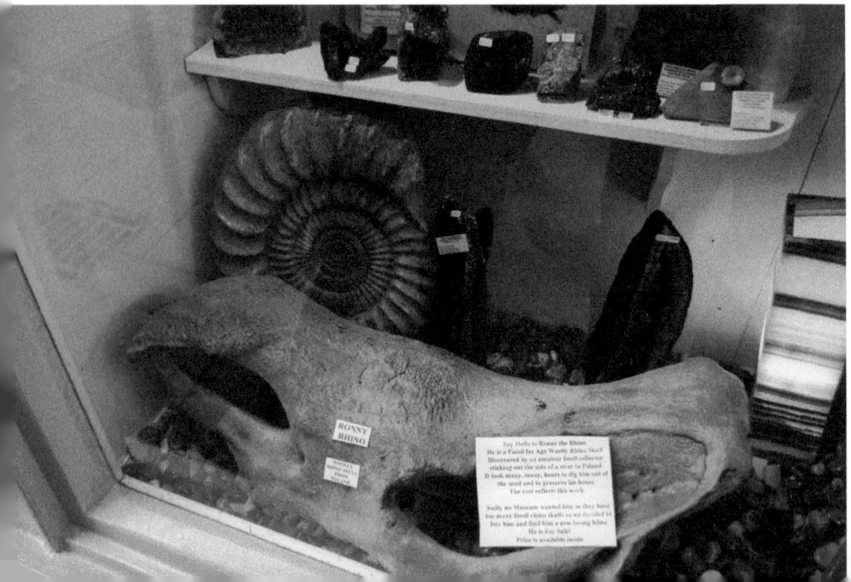

Fossils for sale in a shop on Grape Lane. The cliffs and beaches of Whitby are full of fossils.

G

Gaskell, Elizabeth

Elizabeth Gaskell, otherwise known as Mrs Gaskell, was a successful Victorian novelist. *Mary Barton* (1848), *Cranford* (1853) and *North and South* (1855) are the best known of her works, but Mrs Gaskell is less well known for a book in which Whitby plays a part.

The book is entitled *Sylvia's Lovers* (1863) and it is a much more romantic novel than her earlier works. It is set in Whitby, which Mrs Gaskell renames Monkshaven, but the story is not contemporary with brief visit she made to the town in 1859.

Mrs Gaskell stayed at No. 1 Abbey Terrace on the West Cliff, a property that was part of George Hudson's (the 'Railway King') uncompleted vision for Whitby. The story of the book is based very firmly in the 1790s – days when the town earned its living from the sea, when Monkshaven men crewed the colliers, whalers and fishing boats and when industries such as shipbuilding and sailcloth making were still important.

However brief was her stay, Mrs Gaskell did have an appreciation of Whitby's topography. Early in the novel she describes Monkshaven and she adds that her story is not about the 'local aristocracy', as she calls them, but those who worked in the

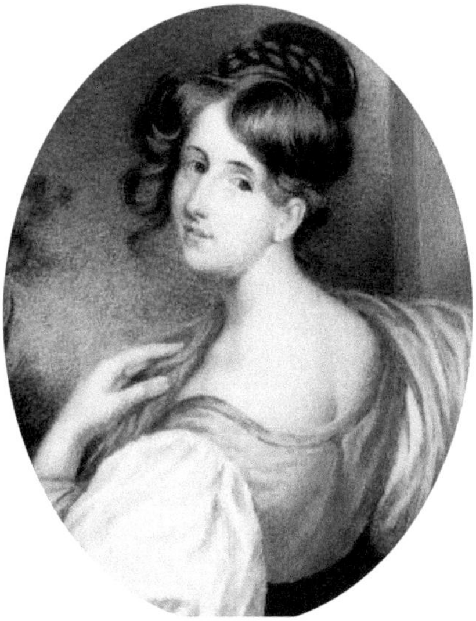

Elizabeth Gaskell, the Victorian novelist, set her story *Sylvia's Lovers* in Whitby. Although the town's name was changed, it is clearly Whitby.

whaling industry. Of course, the novel is aware of the French Revolutionary Wars that are in progress at the time, but it is about what is happening in Monkshaven that interests Mrs Gaskell.

In other words, *Sylvia's Lovers* is as much about personal relationships as it is about historical events. If you have an interest in Whitby, you should read this book and not only for the descriptions of the town. *Sylvia's Lovers* was written over thirty years before Bram Stoker's *Dracula* and some readers might regard that as something of an advantage.

Elizabeth Gaskell, née Stevenson, was born in 1810 in London. She married William Gaskell, a Unitarian minister in Manchester, where she lived, but she did not begin to write until middle age when she published *Mary Barton*. Mrs Gaskell also wrote a famous biography of Charlotte Bronte.

See also: Authors

Ghaut

Several of Whitby's narrow alleyways or 'yards' are also known as ghauts. It would be 'ginnel' in Lancashire. According to Chamber's Dictionary, a ghat, or ghaut (from the Hindi 'ghat', a descent) is an Indian mountain pass carved out by a river, so it may be one of those words that have come to us from India.

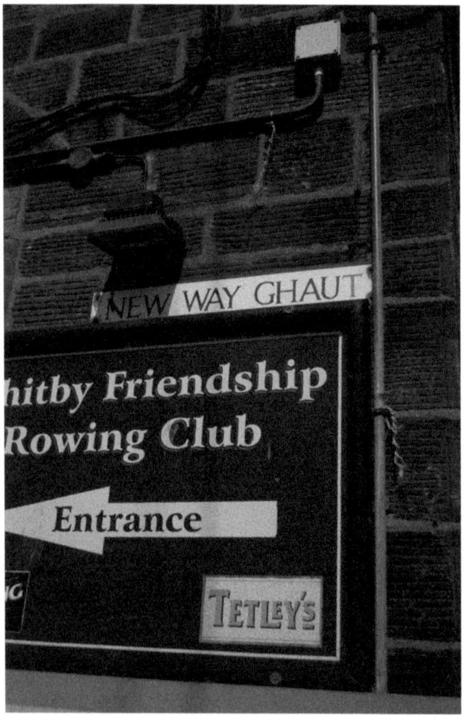

The word 'Ghaut' can be found in various places around Whitby. It refers to a narrow lane leading to the river.

Ghaut may be an ancient word but there is little evidence of that. However, there is a Middle English word 'gote', which refers to a narrow watercourse or channel. That word may have been adapted, in Whitby, to describe a narrow alley which leads to the river. A Whitby glossary of 1855 has an entry for 'gaut' or 'gote' and it was defined as a narrow opening or slip from a street to the river. Two examples are given: Fish Gaut and Horsemill Gaut. The well-known 'ghaut' names in Whitby are Rippon's Ghaut and Tin's Ghaut, both of which are near the river. Lastly, there is a possibility that ghaut is the local pronunciation of 'gate', as in the Norse word gaeta', which means a 'way or a path'.

Ghosts

Whitby, with all its history, has plenty of ghost stories and we could fill an entire book with them, but what we shall do now is give you a taste of some of the creepy tales that give the town its mysterious allure.

To give you an example of how strange goings on take place in Whitby, from the East Pier it is possible to watch the sun rise from behind the abbey and set behind the headland to the left. It is a strange phenomenon as the sun almost appears to be travelling from south to north, not east to west as it should.

Up on the East Cliff we can see the abbey which, it was said, had the most musical bells in the area, if not the World. They were the envy of many and, years ago, an unknown opportunist decided to claim them for himself and organised a raiding party that set sail for Whitby Abbey. The plunderers succeeded in extracting the bells and set sail with their prize. As they turned their ship south, they struck the prominent rock of Black Nab and, weighted down by the abbey bells, the ship sunk to the bottom of the North Sea. If you visit Black Nab at Halloween, in the middle of the dark night you can call out the name of your loved one and you will hear their name echoing back at you on the sea breeze, accompanied by the wedding chimes of the sunken abbey bells.

Whitby has its own musical ghost too. John Metcalfe was born in 1717 in the Yorkshire town of Knaresborough and, at six years old, he lost his sight after contracting smallpox. In order to allow him to be able to make a living, he was given lessons on how to play the violin. John became a highly accomplished player and began to earn money as a travelling entertainer.

Refusing to allow his blindness to hold him back, 'Blind Jack', as he became known, took up swimming, diving, playing cards, gambling, and cockfighting. Following an embarrassing situation involving a couple of women, Jack decided that he should make himself scarce and he left for the North Sea Coast, lodging with his aunt in Whitby and finding work as a violin player.

Blind Jack was later regarded as one of the greatest road engineers of the Industrial Revolution despite his blindness. Many of the roads he built continue to be among the busiest routes in the north of England.

He certainly left his mark, but he also left a legacy in Whitby. At the end of Grape Lane on the east side of Whitby was the site of the Tiger Inn, which could be accessed by a narrow alley known as Cockpit Yard. When Cockpit Yard still stood residents would report that, during the night, they would be woken by the sound of a violin being played in the yard. When they would look out of the window, they would see a ghostly figure with bandages over his eyes playing the fiddle. This apparition would remain in view until some brave soul would venture into the yard to investigate, causing the spirit to vanish.

Not far from Cockpit Yard was No. 17a Grape Lane, once home to the Whitby Photographic Archives, and it has been reported that the ghost of an old sailor has been seen walking along a corridor in the cellar of this old house.

There is also a legend that a sailor from the town who perished would be visited in his grave a few days later by a ghostly coach pulled by headless horses, which would thunder towards the cemetery at St Mary's Church. On board the coach would be a group of skeletal sailors come to pay their respects to their colleague. The coach would then make three laps of the grave, which would cause the ghost to leap from the grave and join the other spectres before disappearing into the night. This fearful tale may have its origins in a much more real setting. It was well known for smugglers to use ghost stories to cover up their activities to keep witnesses away. The coffin of a sailor would make an excellent place to hide smuggled goods and could easily be recovered soon after a funeral.

The Old Smuggler Café, on Baxtergate, dates as far back as 1401 and was once called The Old Ship Launch Inn. Just outside of the Old Smuggler is a carved wooden figure believed to be part of a captured French smuggling vessel, although the facts are now lost in time. The ghost of the Old Smuggler Inn is not a visual apparition but more of an odd presence that announces itself by giving people a gentle push.

These are only a very small number of the ghost stories that give Whitby its mysterious appeal, and the best way to discover more would be to take one of the many ghost walks of Whitby that run most nights from various locations within the town.

See also: Abbey; Authors; Dracula; Grape Lane; Graveyard; Stoker, Bram

Goths

A visitor to Whitby may have noticed that there are some who visit the town dressed in elaborate nineteenth-century costumes with stark make up. These are the celebrated Goths who have adopted Whitby as their spiritual home.

Goths are followers of a particular musical subculture which has its inspiration in nineteenth-century Gothic literature, especially horror novels such as *Dracula*. Indeed, it is acknowledged that the links between Goths and Whitby have arisen from the town's links to Dracula, as well as the accepting nature of the townsfolk.

Twice a year, the Whitby Goth Weekend (an alternative music festival) is held in the town with one of the weekends being held close to Halloween to encourage

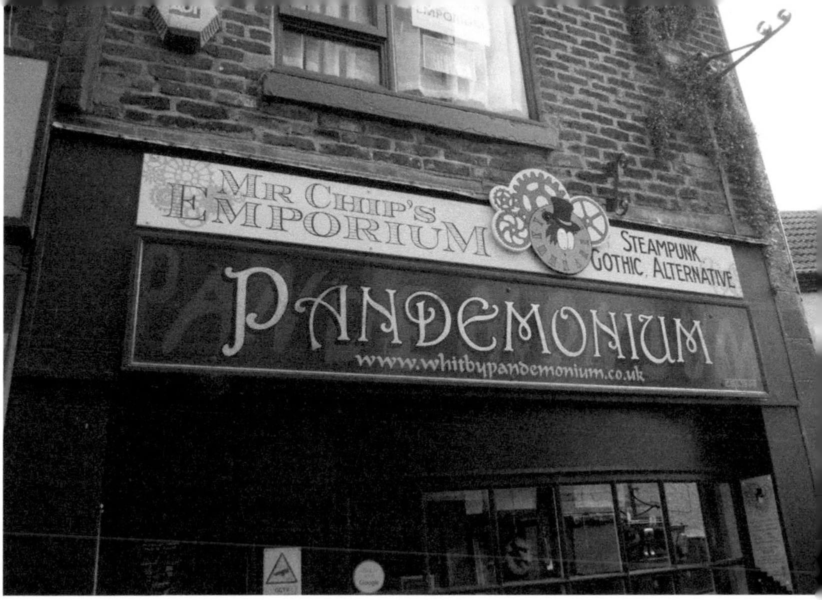

Whitby is also famous for its Goths and there are shops that cater for those who follow that culture.

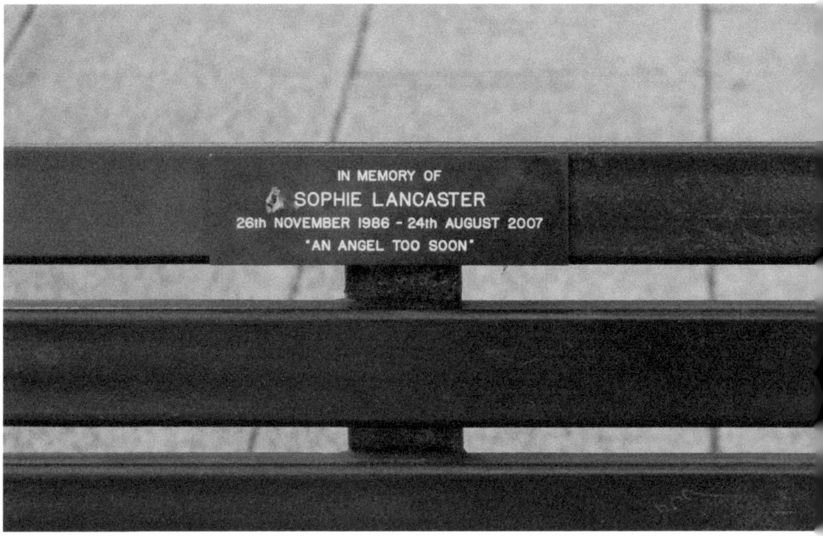

Sophie Lancaster was a Goth who was murdered for being 'different'. A bench dedicated to her memory can be found on Whitby's West Cliff.

more attendance from other subcultures such as vampire aficionados, rockers, and followers of the steampunk culture (a form of alternative science fiction Victorian era, where modern technology is powered by nineteenth-century means). The Goth Weekends are estimated to bring in over £1 million in revenue to Whitby each year with accommodation being at a premium during those weekends.

It is sad to note that Goths have not always been universally accepted outside of Whitby. In 2007 Goths Sophie Lancaster and Robert Maltby were viciously attacked by a group of youths in a park in Bacup, simply because they looked different. Sophie later died of her injuries and, in 2008, a bench in her memory was erected on the West Cliff in Whitby.

In Whitby, however, there is no such prejudice and Goths, and other followers of alternative lifestyles, come together and celebrate being different in a town that means so much to their own culture.

Grape Lane

Grape Lane can be found as you cross the Swing Bridge onto the east side of Whitby. It is the first lane on your right, just next to the Dolphin public house. Today it is a narrow street filled with artisan shops, cafés, restaurants, and other businesses, but, in the past, it was a much seedier location where the pleasures of the flesh could be enjoyed.

Part of Grape Lane was originally known as Tin Ghaut and the car park at the end of Grape Lane is still known as Tin Ghaut car park. The part of Grape Lane where the car park now stands was demolished in 1959. The name is unusual, but it derives from a bit of (possible) Viking language and a bit of Yorkshire dialect. Ghaut is a word for a narrow street or lane leading to a river, and since there used to be an inn at the end of this lane, the Yorkshire dialect for 'the inn' becomes 'T'Inn' meaning the inn at the end of the narrow lane that leads to the river.

Grape Lane itself has an interesting and lurid history behind the name. It used to be known as Grope Lane and some may tell you that it relates to the dark street having no lighting and people would have to grope their way along it. However, during the medieval era, a street name was often known by a defining feature – perhaps it led to a church, and if so, it would be known as Church Street. Or it held a market, as in the case of Market Place. Grope Lane was so named due to it being the hive of prostitution in Whitby and there would have been much groping and fumbling taking place.

In fact, even calling it Grope Lane was an expurgation of a more vulgar name which gave no doubt as to what part of the body was being fondled. This served to confirm that the place was a bawdy and seedy part of town where prostitution was the only trade.

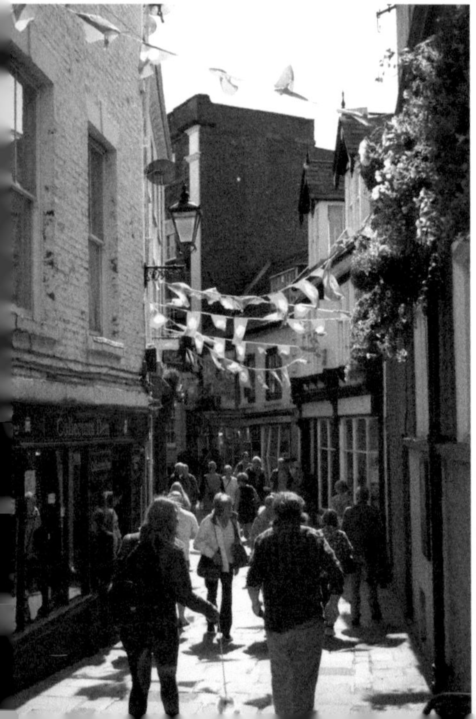

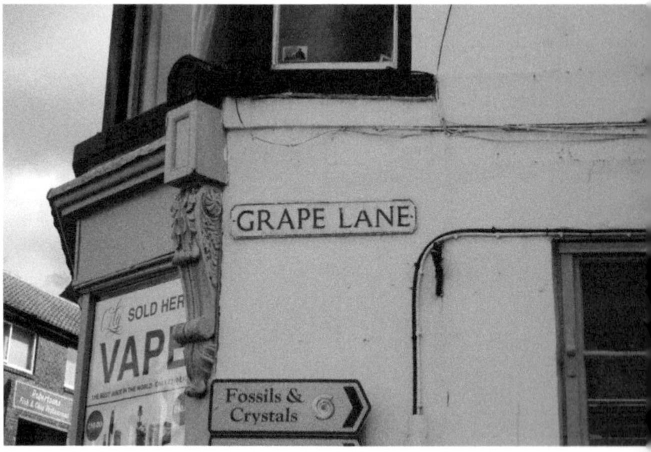

Above: Grape Lane in Whitby was once a seedy and bawdy location famous for its prostitutes.

Left: The Grape Lane of today is a bright and vibrant street with many independent shops and cafés.

As sensibilities changed, Grope was changed to the politer Grape and this is the name that we are left with today. When Captain Cook took lodgings in a Quaker house on Grape Lane, it is unlikely that the street was a den of iniquity at that time and had probably become a more respectful location.

Today Grape Lane is one of the hidden treasures of Whitby. The Coffee Shop does a wonderfully tasting Victoria sponge cake and the restaurants make some of the most satisfying meals you will have in the town. There is a fossil shop, a beer shop, and Captain Cook's old lodgings are now a museum dedicated to his achievements. Grape Lane is well worth the visit, and no embarrassment or damage to your reputation will occur.

See also: Captain Cook

Graveyard

There is more than one graveyard in Whitby, but we are going to look at the most famous one in the town: that of St Mary's, which lies at the top of the 199 Steps. In the past this churchyard was much bigger than it is now; erosion and landslides have taken their toll. Many graves have been lost as the cliff recedes, sometimes leaving a grisly display of coffins poking out of the side of the hill, though these are quickly removed for the sake of dignity.

As you climb up the 199 Steps you will notice some benches placed at various points. These are not benches but 'coffin rests', built for weary pall-bearers as they carried the coffins to the graveyard.

At the top you will see Caedmon's Cross and St Mary's Church, but what is not commonly known is that the churchyard is the resting place of two popular childhood characters: Tom Thumb and Humpty Dumpty. Their graves can be found towards the back of the church in a small area bordered with a low iron fence.

An inspirational view. The graveyard at St Mary's Church has inspired many, not least the author Bram Stoker who set parts of his novel *Dracula* here.

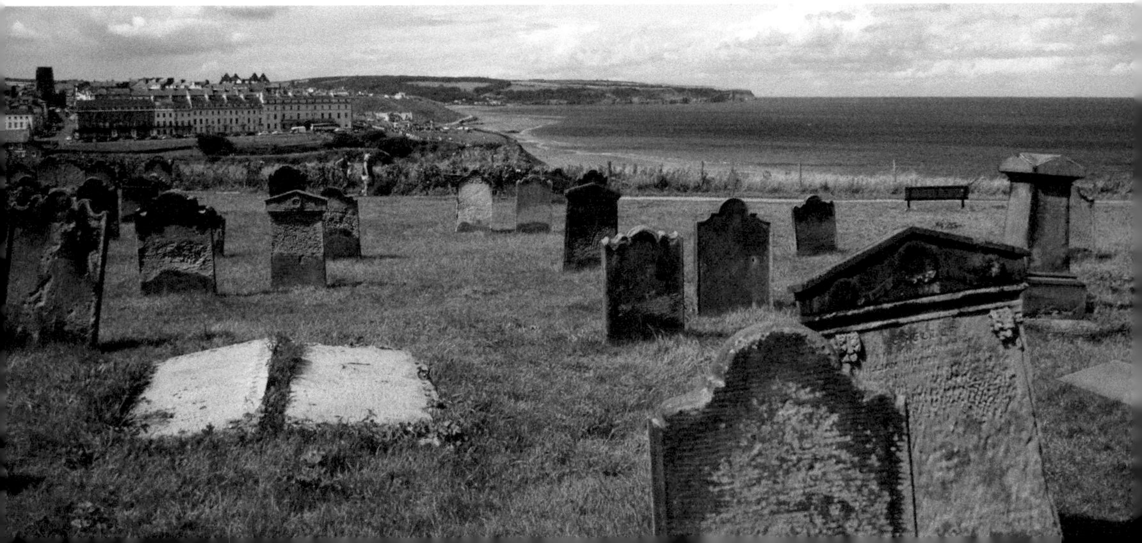

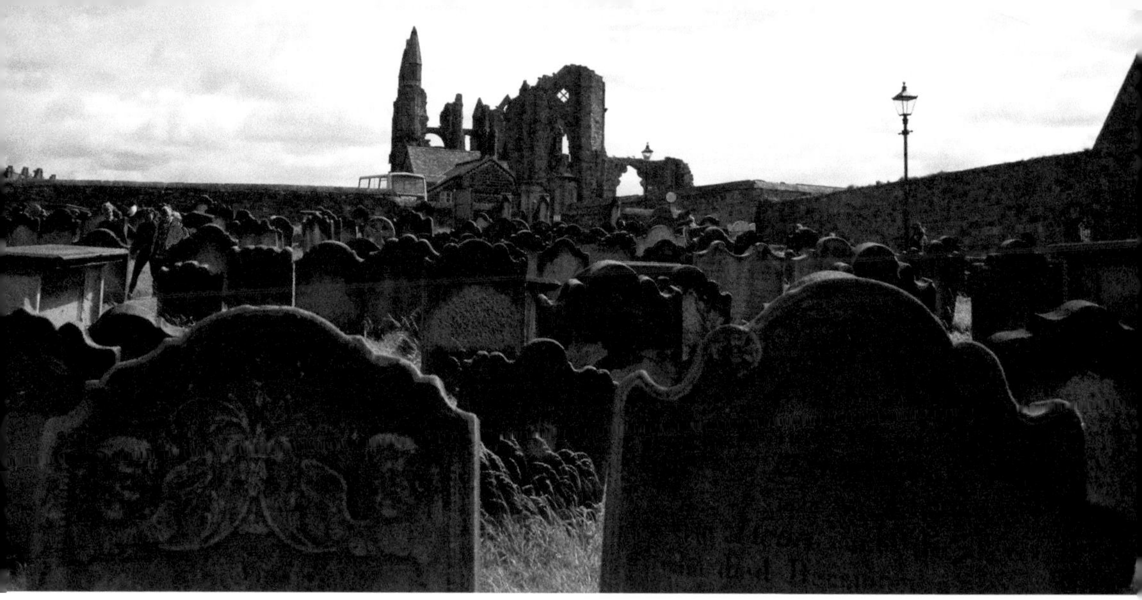

Beyond the graves. The ruins of Whitby Abbey can be found behind the graveyard at the top of the 199 Steps.

Look between two tall graves, side by side, and you will find a tiny headstone, believed by many Whitby children to be Tom Thumb's last resting place. It is probably the grave of an infant between his two parents. Just to the left is a large oval gravestone which, it is believed, holds the shattered pieces of the nursery rhyme character Humpty Dumpty. The sandstone has been weathered to the point where nothing more can be read of the grave. Of course, these are just local tales, told to interest young children, but a few metres away you will find a large, engraved slab set into the alcove above an old and weathered tomb with the following inscription:

> Here lies the bodies of Francis Huntrodds, and his wife Mary, who were both born on the same day of the week, month and year, September ye 19th 1600, married

Below left: The egg-shaped tombstone believed by generations of Whitby children to cover the grave of Humpty Dumpty.

Below right: Is this tiny grave, nestled between two larger stones, the final resting place of Tom Thumb? Or the infant of the couple buried here? The words are long gone so we can only guess.

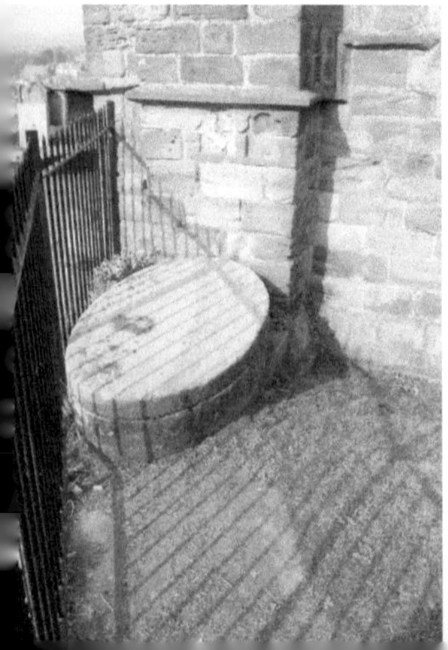

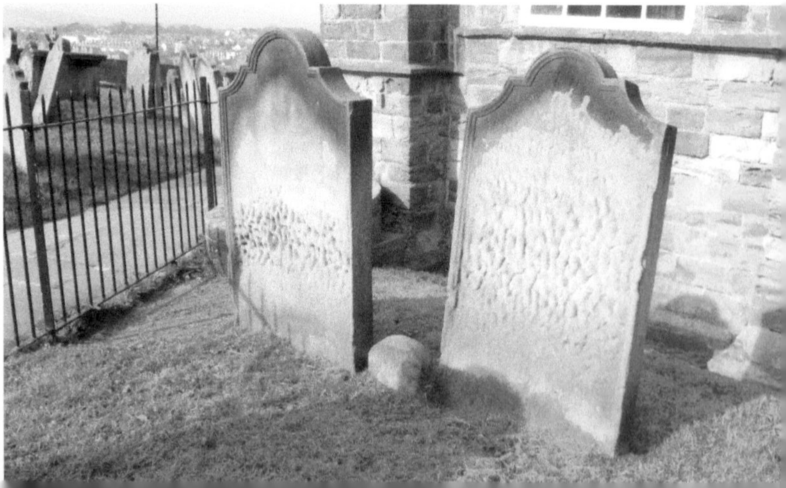

on the day of their birth and, after having had 12 children born to them, died aged 80 years on the same day of the year they were born, ye September 19th 1680 the one not above five hours before ye other.

Husband and wife that did 12 children bare, dyed the same day alike both aged were bout 80 years they lived did part (even on the marriage day) each tender heart so fit a match surely could never be both in their lives and in their deaths agree.

A one in a million occurrence, being born on the same day and dying on the same day. Perhaps Francis and Mary were made for each other?

As you delve deeper amongst the weathered sandstone graves, there is another memorial that might catch your eye. Nestled in a far corner of the churchyard is a grave made entirely of iron. This is the grave of the engineer George Chapman. It is one of only a few metal grave markers in the country. The grave at Whitby was commissioned before Chapman's death and cast at Baxtergate foundry. It has, sadly, fallen into some disrepair and no longer features the iron urn that once topped this impressive memorial.

See also: Dracula, Pirates' Graves

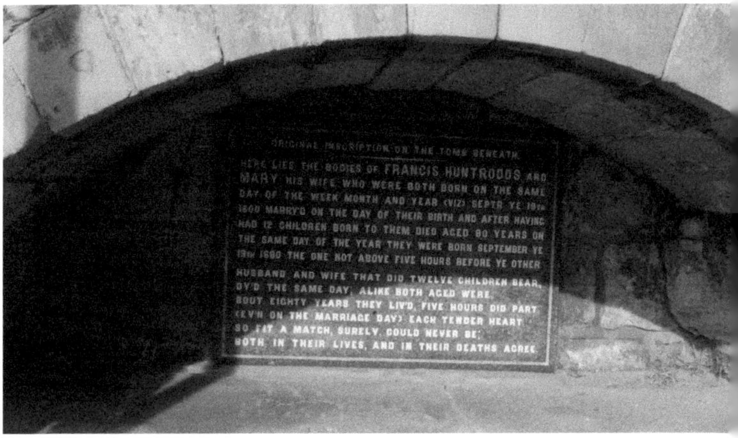

The cryptic Huntrodd's grave detailing a synchronicity that is so strange it can only be true.

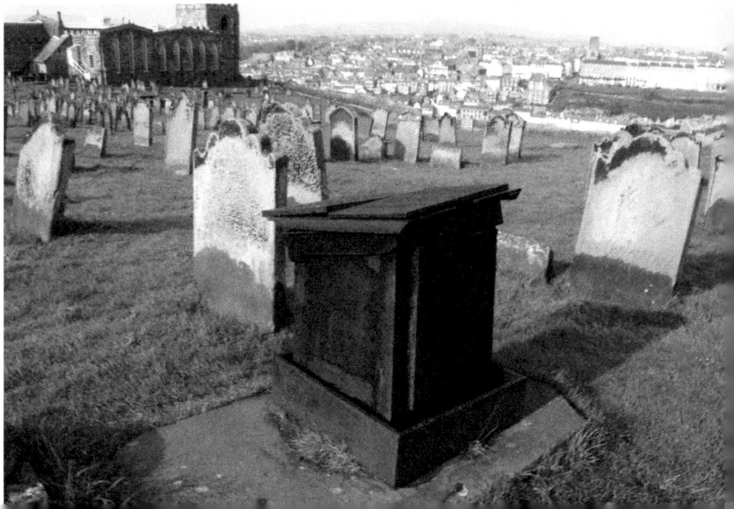

The iron grave of George Chapman, Whitby engineer. Sadly the sea air is taking its toll and it is slowly deteriorating.

H

Hilda

Hilda was born in 614 into the Deiran royal household, her father being the king's nephew. Her father was poisoned when Hilda was very young, so she was raised by King Edwin, who had married a religious woman. This was Aethelburh who, in 627, had the royal court baptised, including Hilda, in a wooden church built near York Minster.

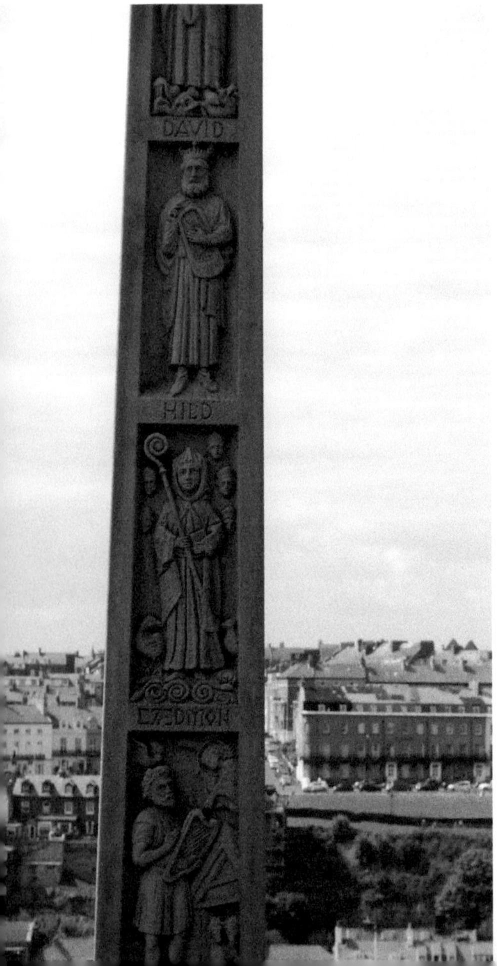

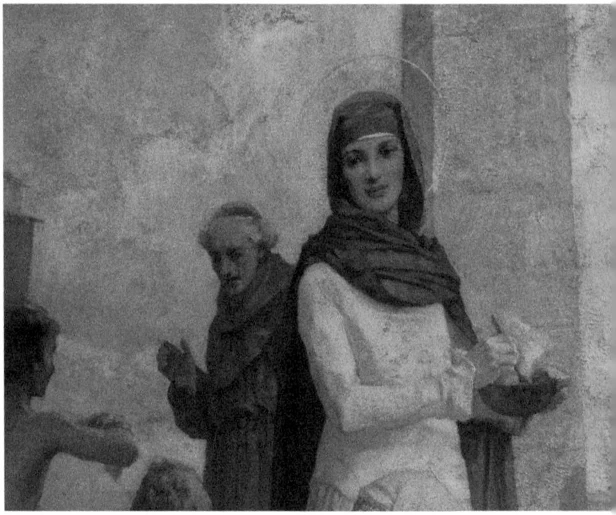

Above: A painting of St Hilda by James Clark.

Left: St Hilda, as carved on Caedmon's Cross in the graveyard on the East Cliff.

In 633 King Edwin was killed in battle and Hilda followed Aethelburh to Kent where the latter founded a convent. Hilda stayed there until she was thirty-three years old and then came back to the north-east of England to live as a nun following the call of Aiden, bishop of Lindisfarne.

Hilda founded her first convent on the banks of the River Wear before Aiden appointed her abbess in a convent that is now lost but was believed to be close to St Hilda's Church in Hartlepool. Then, in 657, Hilda became the founding Abbess at Whitby Abbey and remained there until she died on 17 November 680. She hosted the important Synod of Whitby, which took place in 664.

Hilda was a caring, wise woman with great energy. She was skilled in organising and teaching and, as Abbess of Whitby, she was responsible for a large estate and so had to administer it as well as perform her religious duties. It was Hilda who discovered Caedmon's skill for song.

According to legend, Hilda halted a plague of snakes by turning them into stone. Of course, we know that these as ammonite fossils today, but Hilda's legend was clearly a powerful inspiration as that genus of ammonite is known as *Hildoceras* after her.

See also: Abbey, Ammonites, Caedmon

Hand of Glory

The myths and legends of the Hand of Glory have grabbed the imagination of generations of people, often for its element of gory detail. Whitby has its own Hand of Glory that can be found in the Whitby Museum.

The Hand of Glory is, quite simply, a burglar's tool that has been made from the dried and preserved hand of a hanged man. If it comes from a murderer then,

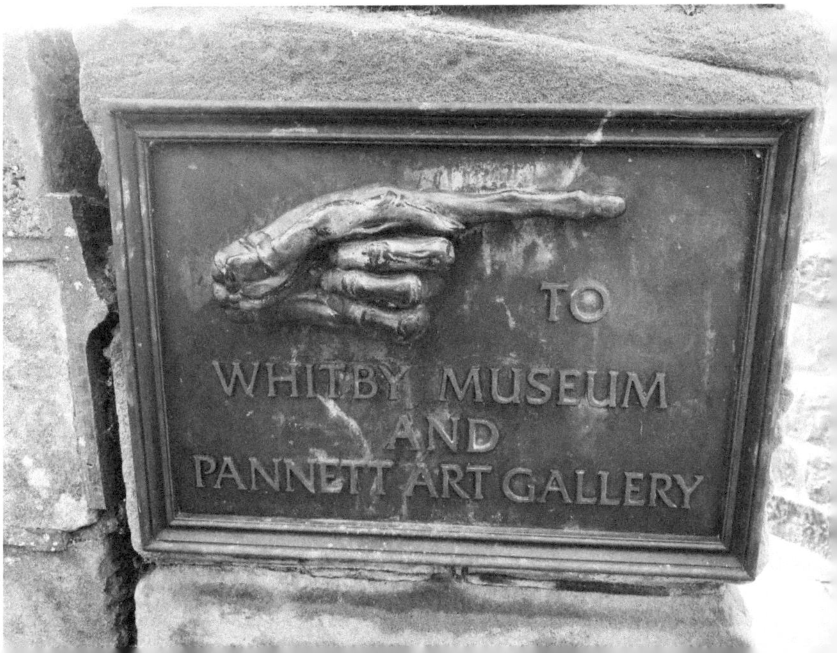

The mysterious Hand of Glory. If you want to see the real thing, follow the finger to Whitby Museum.

ideally, the hand that committed the murder should be selected. This hand should be dried with a mixture of urine, salt and long peppers and left in the sun until totally mummified. The hand, when combined with a candle made from the fat of the hand's donor, will become a powerful magical tool. The candle would be placed into the palm of the hand and the hand would be used like a candlestick. Anyone in the vicinity of this fiendish device (apart from the holder) would become unable to move, sleeping a deep and unnatural sleep. The Hand of Glory was the perfect tool for any burglar.

Whitby Museum's hand was discovered in the parish of Danby, on the North York Moors, in the early twentieth century and given to a mason in the village who was interested in local history and legends. He had heard many stories about the Hand of Glory and the criminal uses made of it, so kept it. The hand is on display in Whitby Museum, in Pannett Park. It is a grisly sight with its long, wrinkled fingernails, and protruding wrist bones and grey-brown skin.

See also: Museum

Home Farm

The Whitby Abbey Home Farm, otherwise known as the Grange, can still be identified, a little over a mile to the south of the abbey, where the site is still marked by its moats, though the buildings have gone. Granges are particularly associated with the Cistercians who assembled the more important of their properties into easily manageable units often at fixed distances (around 25 miles from each other).

Each grange was organised into a team of lay brethren (often as few as two) who were headed by a cellarer. Most granges were farms, often for the rearing of sheep, but at Beaumont, near Lancaster, a grange of Furness Abbey, the income depended on the success of salmon fishing on the River Lune. There is reason to believe that fishing may have been one of the functions of the grange at Whitby.

Hudson, George

George Hudson (1800–71) is known to history as 'the Railway King' because of his financial role in the building of the railway network, a significant part of which he owned. He was born in York serving as a linen draper, until, in 1828, he inherited around £30,000 from his uncle. With this he went into local politics and invested heavily in railways, particularly in Yorkshire. The North Midland Railway became the vehicle for his railway enterprises.

He bought large estates, was three times Lord Mayor of York and was elected MP for Sunderland in 1845. Two to three years later, the 'Railway Mania' of 1847–48 plunged him into debt. He was accused of having fraudulent business books and having paid dividends out of capital. He lost both his fortune and his influence, but Sunderland continued to elect him as the town's MP until 1859.

George Hudson had big plans for Whitby and his influence is still felt in the town. Part of his inheritance included property in Whitby. In addition, he was of the opinion that, with suitable railway connections, the harbour of the town could be extended. He set up the Whitby Building Company and, in the 1850s, it developed the West Cliff area of the town. There is still a Hudson Street in the area, which includes Abbey Terrace. The impressive but incomplete Royal Terrace is to the west of the Captain Cook Monument, and was also one of Hudson's developments.

Of course, much of Hudson's work in Whitby took place after his financial problems were exposed. He had to leave the country, on several occasions, to avoid court action, but he returned to Whitby in 1865 to fight a General Election. In a speech he made at the time, he attacked his opponent, the Liberal MP Harry Thompson, an investor in railways, for failing to link Whitby to the national railway network but achieving the same for rival Scarborough. This went down well with the electors, but he failed to find his way back to the House of Commons.

In his later years, George Hudson was dependent on the charity of his friends, and he died in 1871 without regaining his wealth or influence.

See also: Khyber Pass, Railways, Royal Crescent

Hugh, Earl of Chester

Earl Hugh of Chester, Hugh d'Avranches, is better known as Hugh Lupus (the Wolf, because of his ferocity in battle). He was born *c.* 1047 in Avranches in Normandy, France, and would have been around nineteen years old in 1066 when William the Conqueror defeated Harold II at Hastings.

It is thought that Hugh, who is referred to as Earl Hugh in the Domesday Book, may have been in William's army but, as is often the case, there is no proof of this. He came to prominence in 1071 when he was granted what was to become the great earldom of Chester. He soon established himself as one of the great magnates of Norman England. Hugh had land in around twenty counties, his lands in Yorkshire not being among the most significant. However, much of his Yorkshire property was in the Whitby area and he played an important part in the revival of Whitby, which had suffered greatly during the attacks of the Vikings and, later, the Danes. Several gifts from him resulted in the revival of Whitby Abbey.

Earl Hugh was also known as Hugh the Fat, or, in French, *Hughes le Gros.* He died in 1101 and was succeeded by his son, Richard, who married, Matilda of Blois, the granddaughter of William the Conqueror. Both Richard and Matilda died in the White Ship disaster of 1120, when Prince William, the heir to the throne of England, also died.

I

Industry

There is evidence that the Whitby area may have been settled in Roman times and it is known that there were settlements in and around Whitby during the Dark Ages. Apart from agriculture, one of the first records of industry is that of fishing, which is mentioned by John Leland in in his 'Itinerary' of 1530. (John Chandler's modern translation is used.) Leland writes, 'From Scarborough, eight miles to a little fishing settlement of twenty boats called Robin Hood's Bay, with a haven or bay a mile long; then four miles to Whitby, where there is a large fishing town and a harbour reinforced by a pier.'

Leland gives no details of the size of the Whitby fishing fleet, but it must have been larger than that of Robin Hood's Bay. Whitby was particularly interested in herring and, in 1502, there is mention of a salt house used for salting fish in Whitby. The salting of fish increased in the seventeenth century when several salters established themselves at a place called the 'salt pans', which was located below the East Cliff, probably near Tate Hill Sands. Mention of salt pans may refer, of course, to the industry by which salt was extracted from sea water.

The making of jewellery and other items from jet, which is found locally, became important by the mid-nineteenth century. However, the most significant early land-based industry was the processing of alum, which dates from the sixteenth century. Alum is a double sulphate of aluminium and potassium, which was used as a mordant particularly in the dying of textiles.

In the seventeenth and eighteenth centuries, the growth of Whitby was largely based on alum, as Whitby supplied alum works with coal. The town had no coal of its own but it was obtained from the areas around the Tyne and the Wear. Whitby also became a distribution point for alum and the trade led Whitby into other industrial activities including the building of ships, the making of ropes, sails and sailcloth.

Shipbuilding was a substantial industry by the eighteenth century. In 1802, some thirty-nine vessels were launched in the town, of which the largest was 500 tons, the average for a Whitby ship being 235 tons. Vessels were not only built for the alum industry, but for the coastal coal trade and for whaling.

The ships that carried coal were called 'colliers' and Whitby-built vessels plied the North Sea carrying coal from the north-east of England to London, though other towns and cities on the east coast, without their own coal, participated in this trade.

The ships that were built for whaling had to be particularly strong and Whitby had a number of firms that made vessels for this trade. In 1789, by which time Whitby was becoming a substantial whaling town, there were eighteen vessels employed in this trade. The year 1814 is understood to have been the most successful whaling year when 171 whales were captured.

The coming of the railways in the mid-nineteenth century undermined Whitby's economic role but, by that time, whaling was in terminal decline and shipbuilding was past its peak. Whitby gradually became a visitor attraction, and it has been very successful at that for over 150 years, though some industry remains.

Inns

There are plenty of places at which to quench your thirst in Whitby. The town is fortunate to have plenty of inns and public houses, a feature of places associated with fishing. Whilst describing them all would fill a book, we will look at two of Whitby's pubs, both of which have an interesting history.

The White Horse and Griffin is on Church Street. It was built in 1861 by Sir Hugh Cholmley as a coaching inn for the Whitby-York-London route as well as a meeting place for Captain Cook and William Scoresby who would hire their crews from the inn. The pub's name comes from the Cholmley coat of arms, which bears a white horse and griffin.

The inn closed in December 1939 at the commencement of the Battle of the River Plate, the first major sea battle of the Second World War, which, incidentally, used to be regularly re-enacted at the lake at Peasholm Park in Scarborough. The White Horse and Griffin didn't open again until 1993 and since then it has played host to several celebrity guests.

Just down the road is a very similar inn called the Black Horse, which was also a coaching inn and was originally known as the White Horse (again, from the Cholmley coat of arms). If you think that having two pubs on the same street with very similar names was confusing, you'd be right. But there was some benefit to this confusion in an elaborate scam involving both inns.

In the eighteenth century it was common practice to send a letter ahead to a coaching house. The letter would contain a banknote, which would be used for payment for food and lodging. The letter would be addressed simply to 'The White Horse'. The traveller would arrive to find that his letter, and his funds, were nowhere to be seen. He would have to pay for stay.

The day the payment was made, the traveller would be sent to a lawyer (also in on the scam), who would point out that the letter had been sent to 'an inn with the

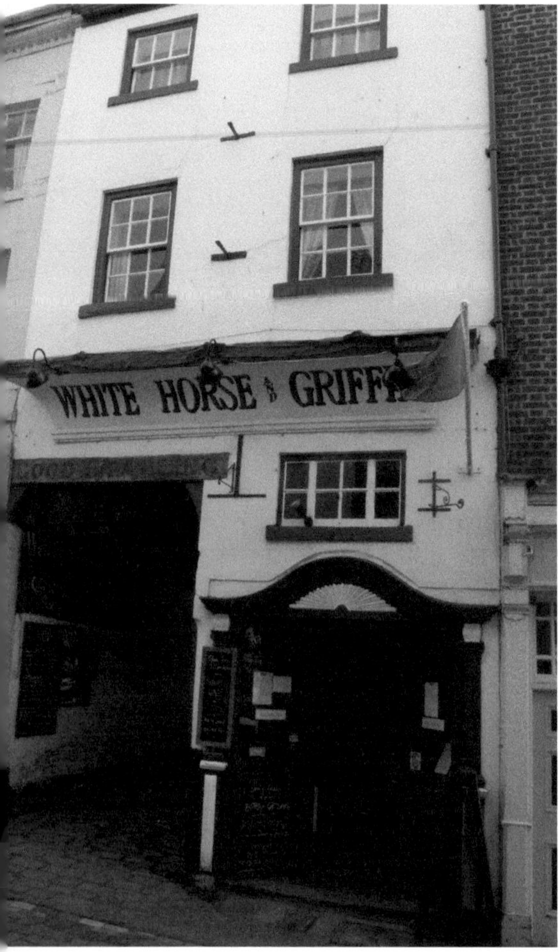

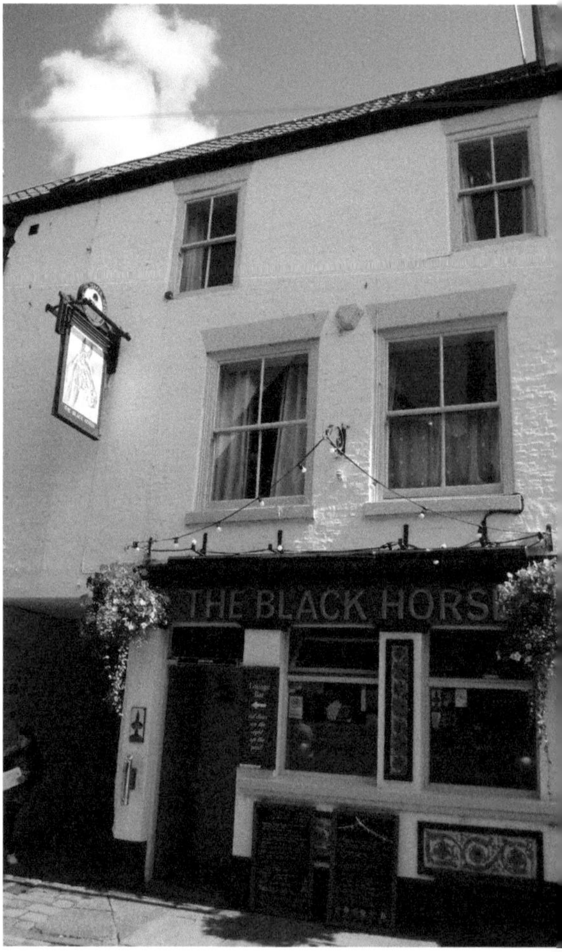

Above left: The White Horse and Griffin that takes its name from the coast of arms of the Cholmley family.

Above right: The Black Horse Inn – originally called the White Horse but forced to change its name to bring to an end a scam that lasted over 100 years.

similar name' whilst the traveller had gone 'to the other inn'. The lawyer would then present the infuriated traveller with a bill for his services! This scam went on for over a hundred years and ended when a magistrate decided that enough was enough. Innocent people should not be taken advantage of and he decreed that the White Horse should change its name or lose its licence. In 1828, the White Horse became the Black Horse Inn.

J

Jet

If you have a taste for jewellery, how about something that has literally taken millions of years to produce? You may have noticed, as we have made our way around the town, something called Whitby Jet. It is carved into decorative shapes and used to make lavish and beautiful pieces of jewellery, but why is it so important in Whitby?

Fossils made Whitby famous but jet is another fossil. It is the black remains of a Jurassic plant which is like the Monkey Puzzle Tree seen in gardens all over the country. Jet is approximately 182 million years old and, although it can be found worldwide, it is thought to be superior in Whitby because of the effects of compression and salty water.

Jet has been used as a form of jewellery since Neolithic times. In the Bronze Age, it was used to make beads for necklaces, and the Romans adopted it as a fashion item before it fell out of favour until the Victorian era when its popularity returned.

The words are barely visible now, but this shows that their jet was a significant business in Whitby.

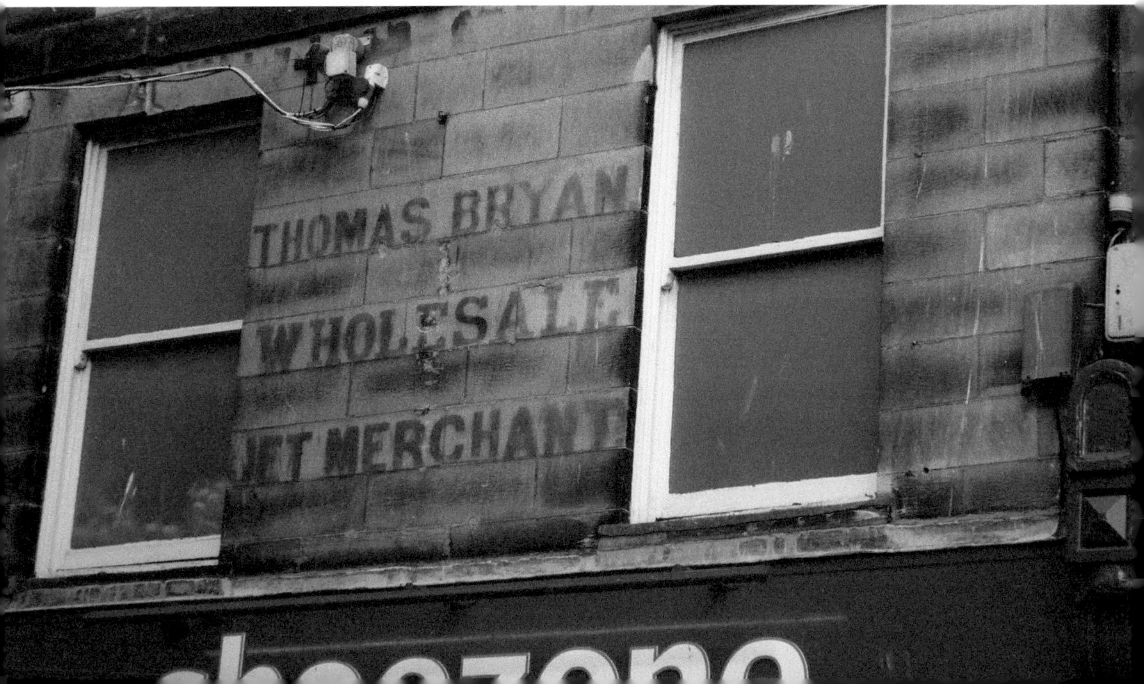

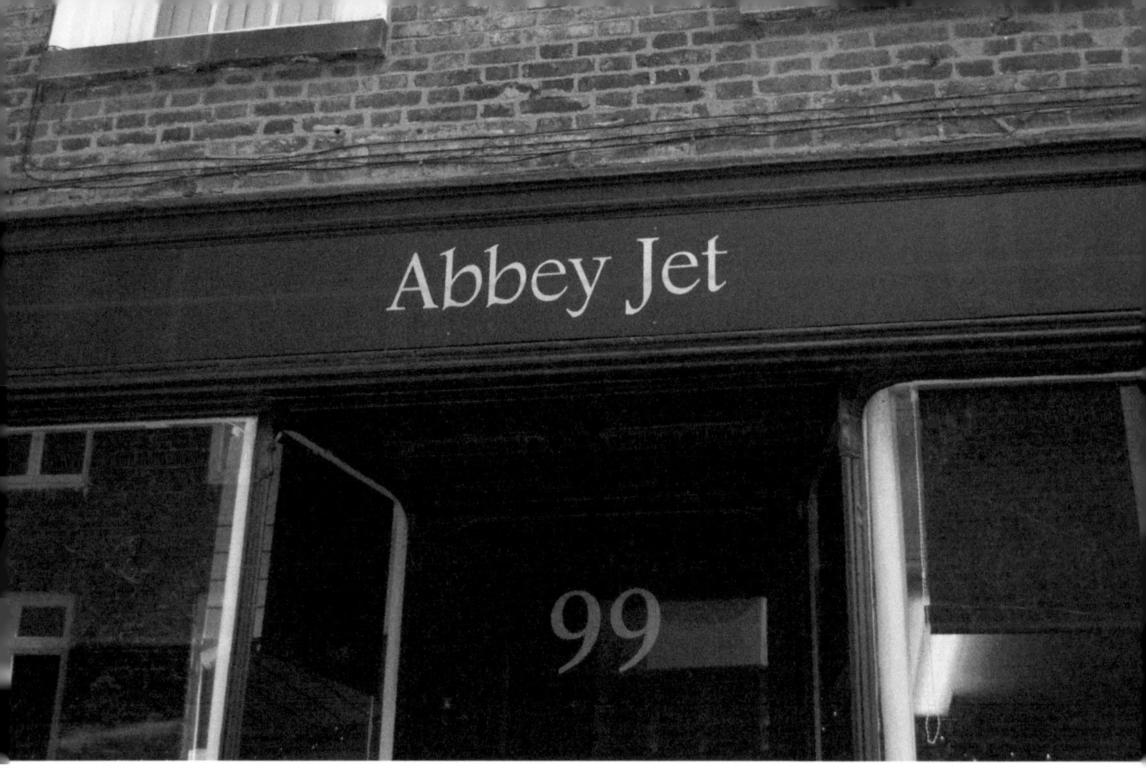

A Whitby Jet merchant. The town is still famous for hand-crafted jet jewellery.

When Prince Albert died, Queen Victoria wore black to indicate that she was in mourning. This extended to her jewellery, which was made from Whitby Jet. The Queen's jewellery was an instant hit with Victorian society, who wanted to imitate her look.

Today, especially on the east side of Whitby, you will find many shops that specialise in Whitby Jet jewellery and many of these still retain their traditional workshops. In addition, the Whitby Jet Museum can be found at the foot of the 199 Steps, where jet has been turned into jewellery since 1860.

See also: Fossils, Victorians

K

Khyber Pass

Whitby's Khyber Pass is a winding road flanked steeply on both sides that meanders from the West Pier to the top of the West Cliff. It was named after the famous mountain pass on the Pakistan and Afghanistan border that was, for hundreds of years, an important trade route. At the top of the Khyber Pass is the start of a series of terraces. East Crescent becomes East Terrace, then turns left onto North Terrace and, a short distance along, we come to partly completed Royal Crescent. This was the result of

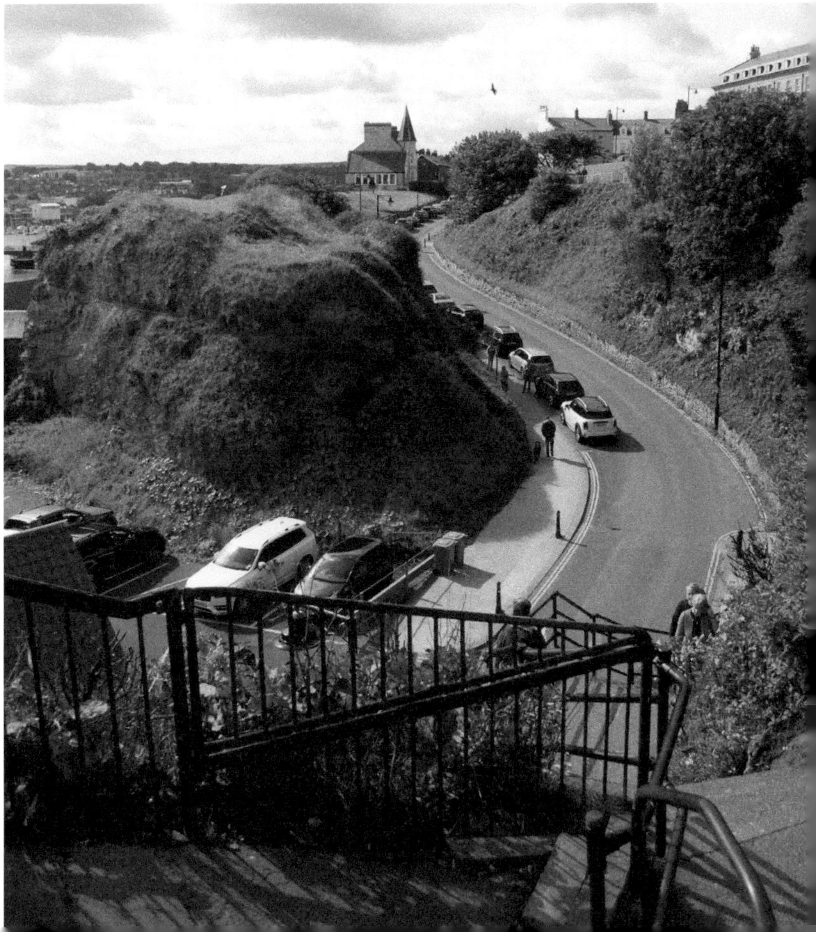

The winding road, carved out of the cliff, is said to resemble the famous Khyber Pass. It was used to transport building materials up the cliff.

George Hudson's bankruptcy. But Royal Crescent would not have existed had it not been for the Khyber Pass. Hudson needed to find a way to easily transport building materials to Royal Crescent from the town's train station, so he had the Khyber Pass dug out of the cliffs in order to facilitate this.

This remarkable feat of civil engineering might have served a utilitarian purpose but it is now one of Whitby's best-loved landmarks. There is the row of benches along the top of Spion Kop, on the Pass's left side, where you can sit and admire the view over the harbour, or you can climb the steps on the right side of the Pass to reach the Whalebone Arch on the top of the West Cliff. Whichever way you choose, there's no denying that the Khyber Pass offers some of the best views of Whitby.

See also: Hudson, George; Railway; Royal Crescent

Kippers

If you were to stand at the foot of the 199 Steps, you might notice an interesting and tantalising smell wafting down Henrietta Street – a smoky smell, with a pleasant hint of cooked fish, which starts your mouth watering. Around halfway up Henrietta Street

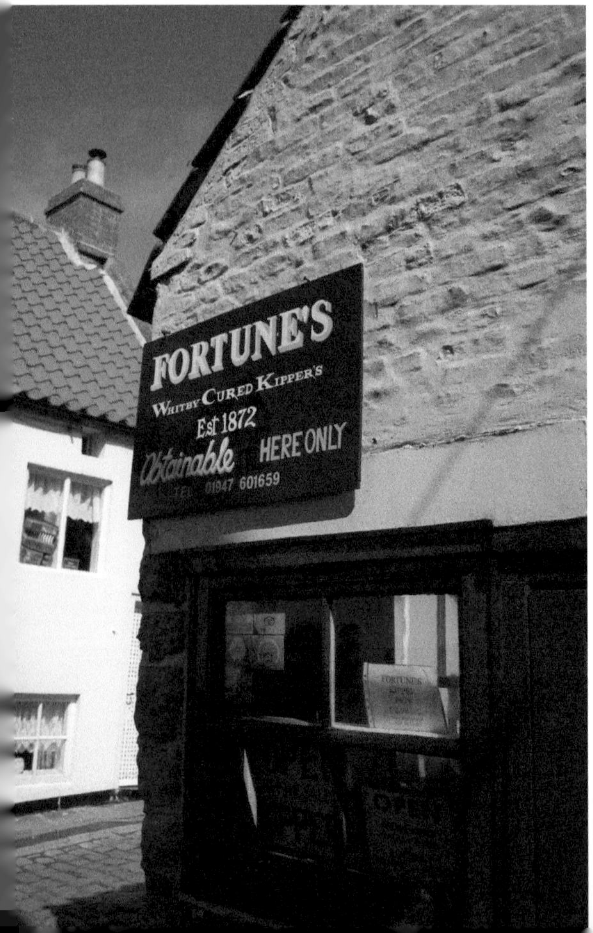

Fortune's – Whitby's only traditional smokehouse.

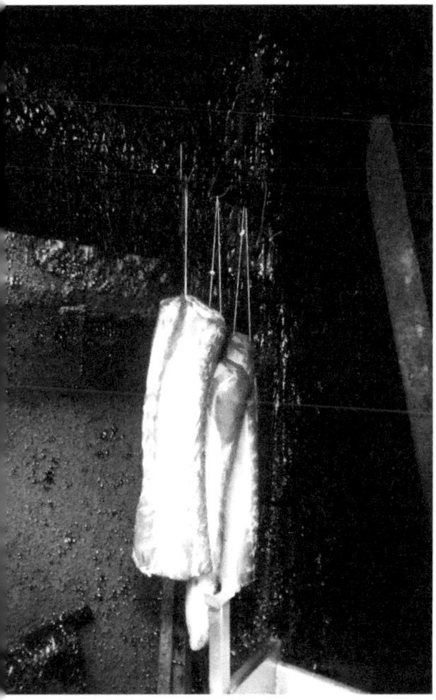

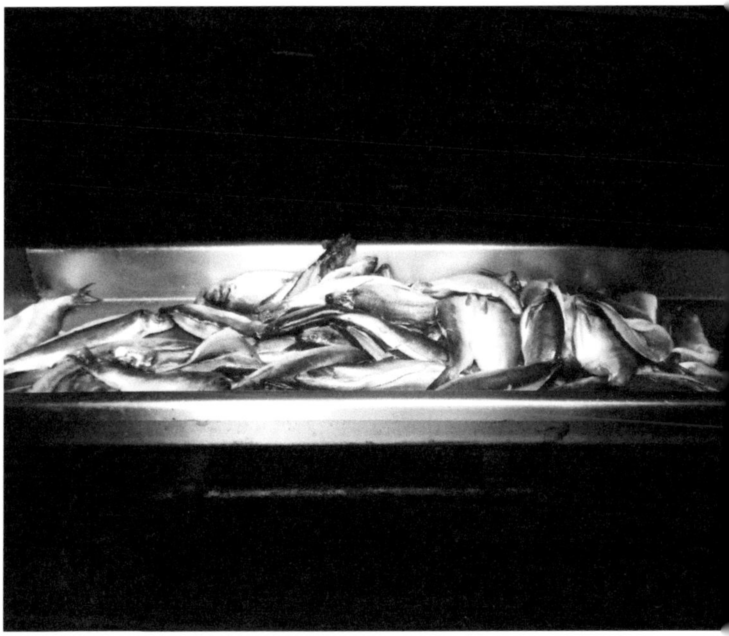

Above left: Meat hangs in the smokehouse. Note the tar-like deposits on the walls – the by-product of smoking.

Above right: These herrings have been gutted and split and await hanging in Fortune's smokehouse. The end product will be the famous Whitby Kippers.

is a small, single-storey shop, Fortune's, which is Whitby's only surviving traditional smokehouse. The firm is famous for its kippers.

Kippers are herrings that have been split from head to tail and gutted by hand. At Fortune's, the kippers are then brined for forty minutes to improve the flavour, before they are slow smoked over oak, beech and softwood.

Fortune's has remained a family business since it was established in 1872 and shows no sign of breaking that lineage. Boasting customers from the British royal family and celebrity chefs, this is truly the perfect place to try kippers if you are yet to experience them.

See also: Fishing

L

Lifeboats

Being a town with a reliance on the sea, it is only to be expected that there is a need for a lifeboat, and Whitby has strong links to the brave men and women of the Royal National Lifeboat Institution. Whitby lifeboats have been helping those in peril for over 200 years and the crews of those boats have been decorated for bravery thirty-six times.

Whitby lifeboats have been pioneers, having the first lifeboat station of its kind, which was built in 1802. Since then, there have been four lifeboat stations in Whitby, two of which survive. One is on the west side, and is now the lifeboat museum, and the other is a motor lifeboat station on the east side, which opened in 1919.

In 1862 tragedy struck the crew of the Whitby lifeboat when it was launched to save vessels in distress during a fierce storm. The lifeboat launched five times and on the fifth, the lifeboat was capsized and twelve of the crew were drowned. The only survivor was Henry Freeman who was wearing a cork life vest. A memorial to the

Below left: The gravestone lists those lost in the Whitby lifeboat disaster of 1861. All but one of the crew was lost.

Below right: The former Whitby lifeboat the *Mary Ann Hepworth* now takes tourists on trips from the harbour.

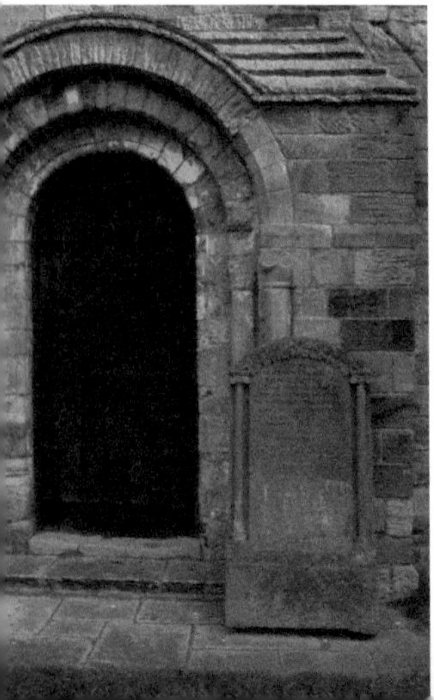

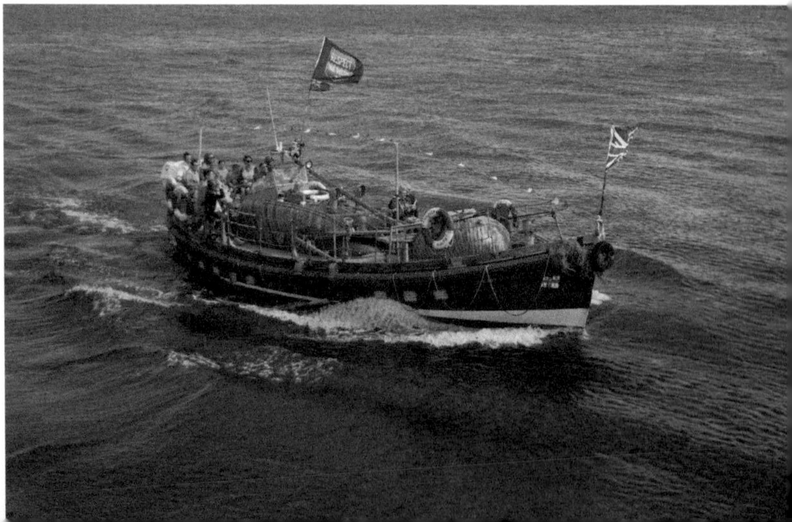

lost lifeboat men can be seen at St Mary's Church. After this incident the Whitby lifeboat came under the control of the RNLI (it had previously been part of the Whitby Lifeboat Institution) and a new lifeboat was provided.

In 1914 one of the greatest rescues in lifeboat history took place off Whitby when the hospital ship *Rohilla*, making for to Dunkirk, struck a reef and broke in two. Lifeboats from up and down the north-east coast were launched and one of Whitby's vessels was lowered down the cliff in an attempt to save those trapped on the wreck. Three days later the rescue was over, with 144 people saved.

The *Rohilla* incident heralded the dawn of the motor lifeboat era. In 1938, the lifeboat the *Mary Ann Hepworth* started in service. Today it is possible to take trips out of the harbour on *Mary Ann* as she now works as a tourist boat and gives an invaluable insight into what it would have been like for the crews on those boats.

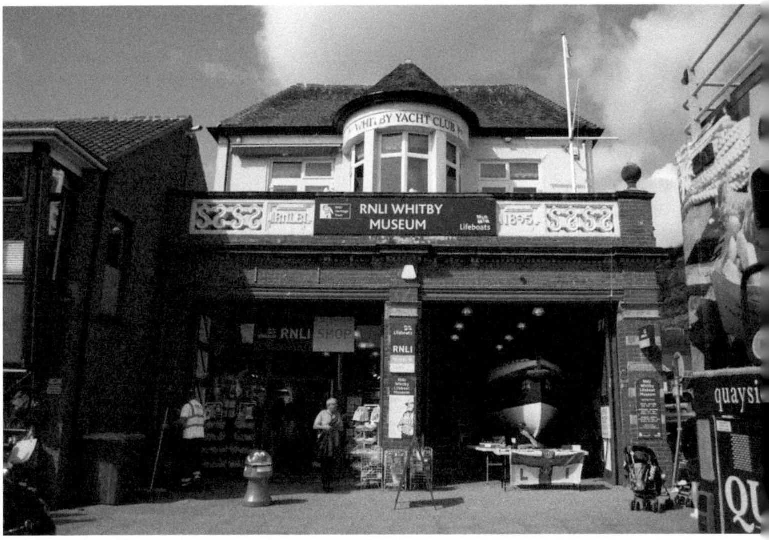

The old lifeboat station is now a museum chronicling the history of Whitby's lifeboats.

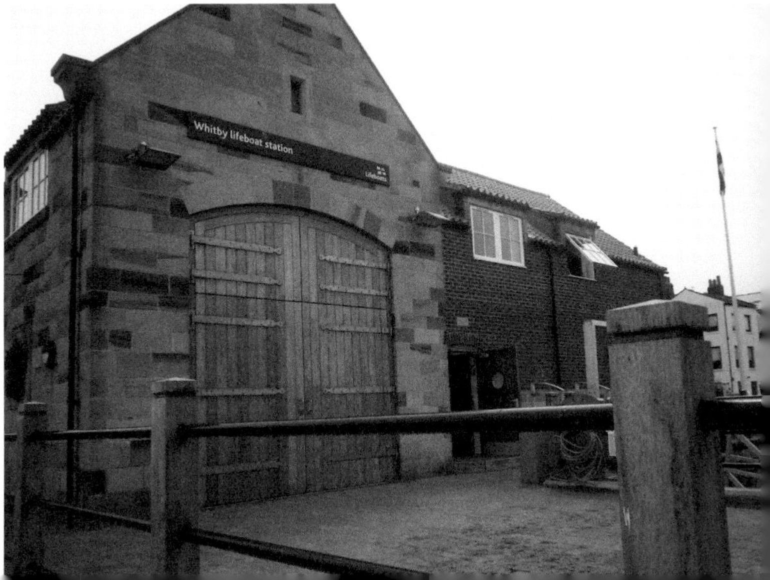

The new lifeboat station sits at the foot of the East Cliff.

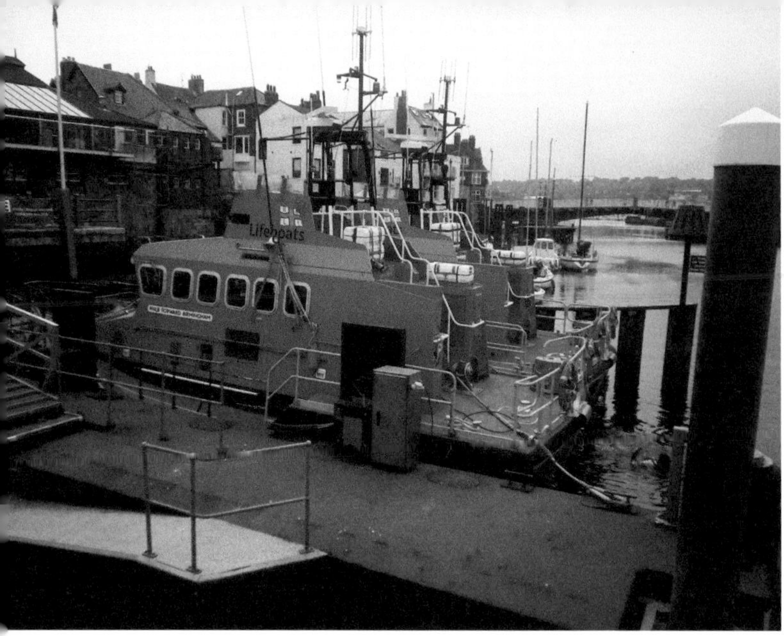

The crews of Whitby's lifeboats have been saving lives for over 200 years and received gallantry awards thirty-six times. Here we see two Trent class lifeboats at Whitby lifeboat station and one lifeboat man swimming behind them!

It is also well worth paying a visit to the lifeboat museum where you will see displays and artefacts from Whitby's proud lifeboat history. It is also worth remembering that the RNLI costs £163.5 million per year to run and that money comes from the public who support it through donations. It is run separately from the coastguard and is independent from the government so, if you can, please help support the great work they do.

Lighthouse

There is evidence to suggest that there was a lighthouse in Whitby in Roman times. If so, it would have been situated close to the abbey and its existence would suggest that the harbour of Whitby was being protected to assist shipping.

Today, Whitby is instantly recognisable by its two piers that sweep out into the harbour. The piers are Grade II listed, and in 2018 underwent urgent work to repair them from the ravages of the sea and bad weather. On each pier is a lighthouse and if you were to look at the West Pier lighthouse you will see the result of two centuries of bad weather on the sides of the it. The sandstone blockwork is ridged and scarred by sand, sea and strong winds, which have eroded the stone.

Today the West Cliff lighthouse operates as a tourist attraction and it is possible to climb the winding stairs to the top where a wonderful vantage point awaits you. The West Cliff lighthouse also has its own ghost; that of a lighthouse keeper who, one stormy night, set out to keep the light illuminated. He struggled up the winding steps and lit the light and then, as he turned back to descend the stairs, fell on the steps that had been made slippery by the storm. Down and down he fell until he reached the door at the bottom and broke his neck.

The East Pier has no such ghost and is 30 feet lower than its companion, but it is the Whitby lighthouse on the East Cliff that now protects seafarers from the coast. Built in 1857, and made operational a year later, the lighthouse is an octagonal white tower.

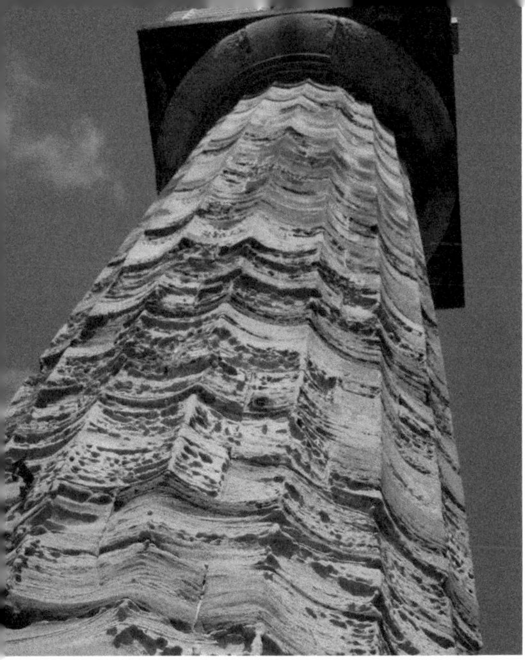

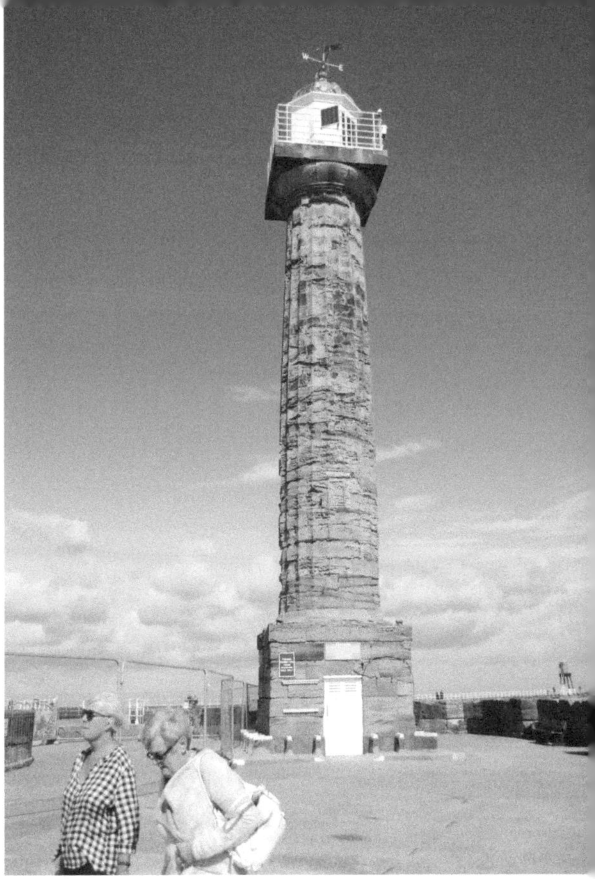

Above: The sandstone of the lighthouse has been eroded by the sea for generations, resulting in these strange formations.

Right: The West Pier lighthouse is the tallest of the two. It is possible to climb to the top of it.

It was once the shorter of a pair of towers that would be lined up, in transit, to identify a significant shipping hazard, that of Whitby Rock.

In 1890, the lighting system was improved, which meant that the taller tower was decommissioned and, ultimately, demolished to allow for the fog-signalling building to be constructed. The new building featured two huge trumpets that bellowed, like a wounded bull, in foggy conditions, earning the signal the nickname 'The Hawsker Bull' (Hawsker is a nearby village).

Through time the lighthouses have helped ships pass through the piers.

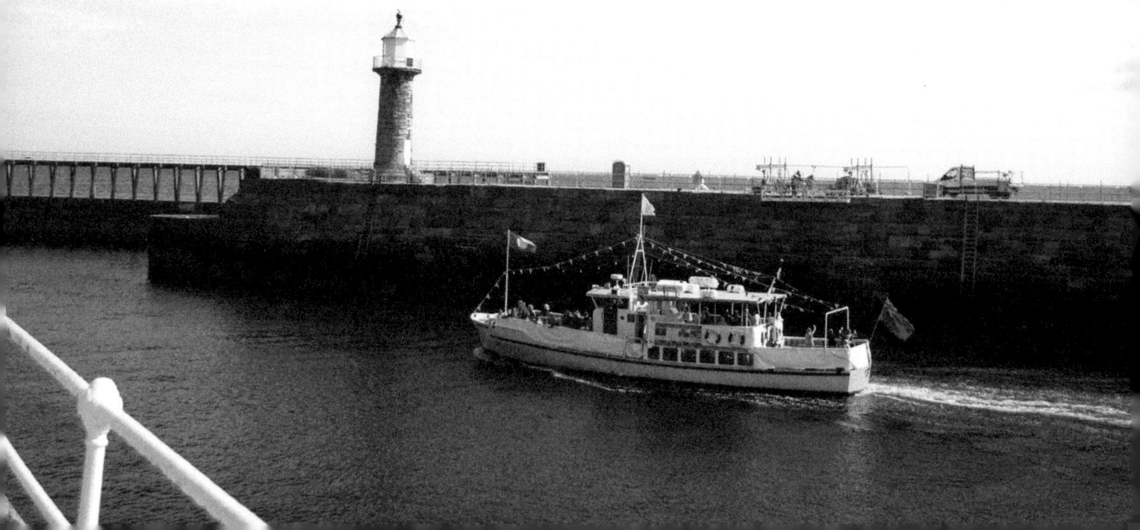

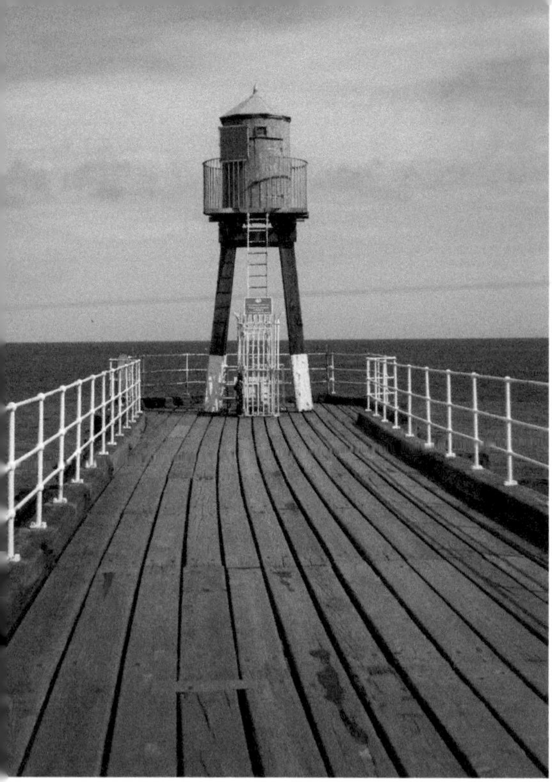

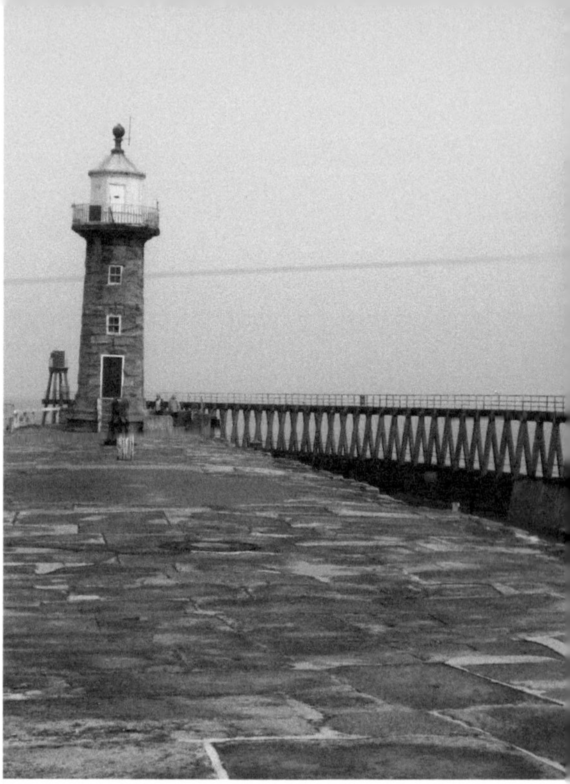

Above left: The green beacon tells shipping that this is the starboard (or right) side of the harbour.

Above right: The East Pier lighthouse.

The Hawsker Bull was in service until 1988 when it was replaced by an electric foghorn. The lighthouse was also electrified in 1972 (having run on paraffin before that) and became fully automated in 1992. Today the lighthouse continues to keep ships safe from harm and, on a foggy morning, the new foghorn sends its eerie warning across the sea to complement the lighthouse.

The opposite beacon is red, signifying the port (left) side of the harbour.

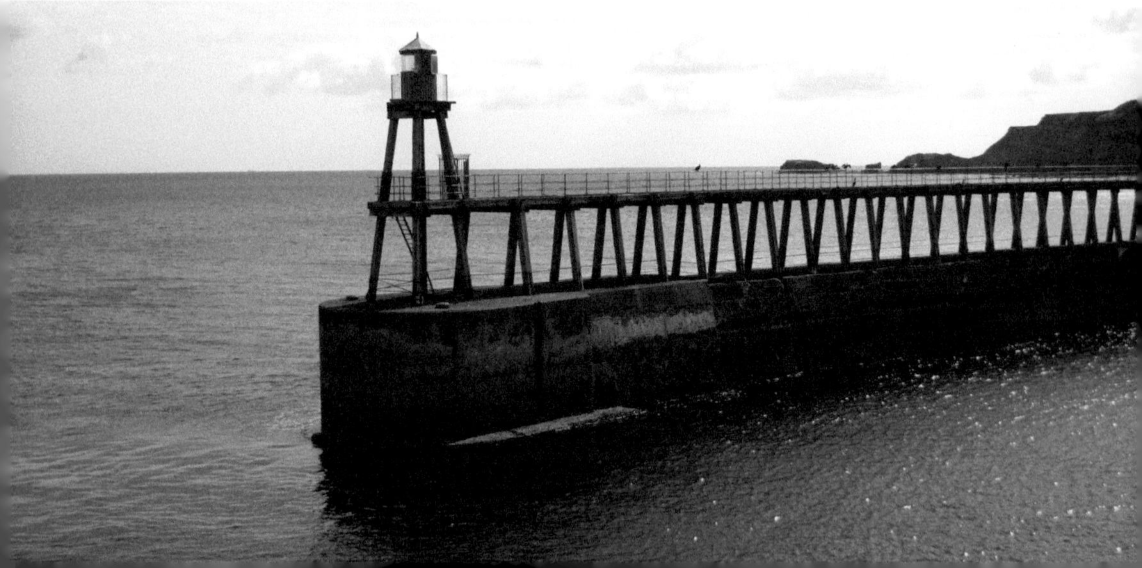

M

Maharajah

As you drive out of Whitby towards Sandsend you may notice a lonely little house opposite the golf course. It was once a toll house and collected its last fee in 1925 before becoming a private house. It has an interesting history as it was built in the 1860s under the instructions of Indian Maharajah Duleep Singh.

Duleep was born in September 1838 and was the last maharajah of the Sikh Empire, succeeding when he was five years old. Following the First Anglo-Sikh War, he was separated from his mother and was placed in the care of Dr John Login, who was responsible for his education.

By the time he was fifteen, Duleep had converted to Christianity and in 1854, he was exiled to England where he became something of a novelty in the royal household and was a frequent guest of Queen Victoria.

Shortly afterwards, Duleep moved to Scotland where he would dress in Highland costume and stalk the moors dressed as a Scottish laird. This lasted for a few years and then he returned to England and took out a lease on Mulgrave Castle, just outside of

Below left: The toll road to Sandsend, built by the Maharajah Duleep Singh.

Below right: Duleep Singh, Whitby's own maharajah.

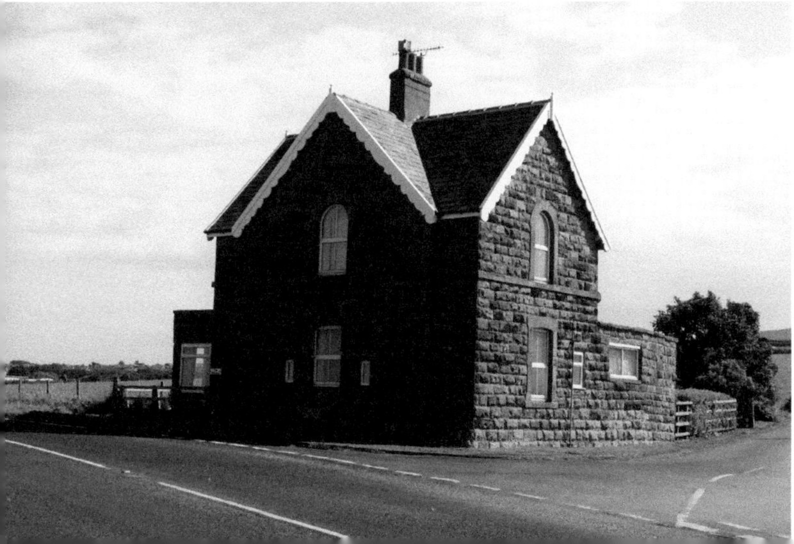

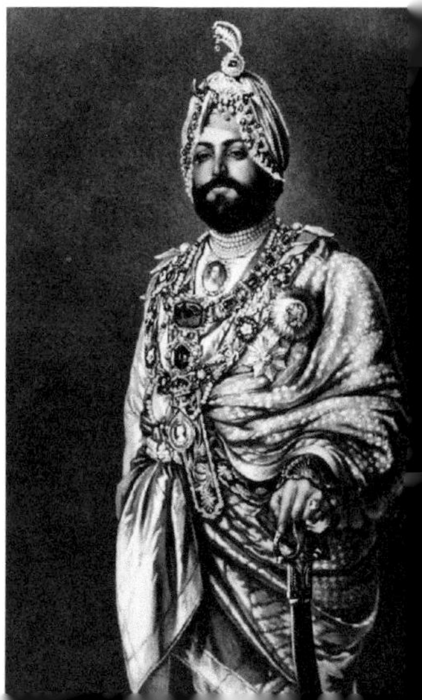

Whitby. It is rumoured that he and his retinue would travel along the beach to Whitby on the backs of elephants. Duleep, it is said, was worried about the sand hurting the toes of the elephants' feet and so constructed the Sandsend to Whitby road to make the journey easier for them.

There is, sadly, no evidence to suggest that Duleep Singh ever kept elephants at Mulgrave Castle and it is thought that it is a nice little tale made up to explain an old photograph of two elephants on the beach at Whitby, which, in all probability were from a travelling circus.

Duleep had been very wealthy at one point, even gifting the famous Koh-i-Noor diamond to Queen Victoria, but he lost his fortune and died from an epileptic fit in a Paris hotel in 1893.

See also: Mulgrave Castle

Mulgrave Castle

These days the estate, of around 15,000 acres, at Mulgrave Castle is not normally opened to the public but it is noteworthy because the owner of the castle may have been involved in one of England's most enduring historical mysteries, one which rivals, for interest, the disappearance of the Princes in the Tower in the reign of Richard III.

At Mulgrave there have been three significant properties but there could have been four. The first of these may have been a Roman structure, as building materials from that time have been found incorporated into the probable third building on the site, which is known as the Old Castle. The ruins of this building are likely to have had Norman origins, but they were slighted, on the orders of Parliament, after the Civil War in the seventeenth century.

Of the second building there are, apart from ditches and mounds, no substantial remains, but it is thought that it may have been a fort associated with Duke Wada, who lived in the eighth century. The last building at Mulgrave, potentially the fourth, is the present country house, which was built by Lady Catherine Darnley, who was the illegitimate daughter of King James II and wife of John Sheffield, first Duke of Buckingham and Mulgrave. The estate passed to the Phipps family, who are still in possession, though it was famously leased to Duleep Singh, the last maharajah of the Punjab, in 1858.

The mystery dates to the early thirteenth century but it is also a murder mystery. One of the builders of the first castle, potentially the third building on the site, Robert de Turnham, left no male heirs, so the estate passed to his daughter, Isabel, who was made a ward of King John. Although John succeeded his brother, Richard I (the Lionheart), it is not generally realised that John, in some respects, was not Richard's heir. That was Prince Arthur, the son of John's older brother, Geoffrey, who had died in an accident in a tournament in 1186.

When Richard I became king in 1189, he acknowledged Prince Arthur as his heir, rather than his younger brother, John, but Mulgrave Castle comes into the story through Peter de Maulay, who married Isabel, the heiress to the castle, when John had secured the throne in 1199. The price is said to have been the murder of Prince Arthur, which may have happened in 1203.

There is no proof that Peter de Maulay was the murderer, but nothing is heard of Arthur after the prince fell into the hands of King John, who imprisoned him, first at Calais and then at Rouen in France. John may have been the murderer. There are accounts of him carrying out the act with his own hands and disposing of the body into a French stream, but is possible that John had Arthur murdered at Rouen and that de Maulay was the agent of his death.

It is known that de Maulay was, at one time, Governor of Corfe Castle, in Dorset, where Arthur's sister, Eleanor, was kept in captivity by king John. It is understood that this was done to prevent her from producing a male heir who might claim John's throne.

See also: Maharajah

Museums

If history is your thing and you want to delve deep into the past, then Whitby has two great museums. The Captain Cook Museum is in Grape Lane, and here you can find out more about the great seafarer.

The Whitby Museum is in Pannett Park and has been there since 1931. It is run by the Whitby Literary and Philosophical Society, which was founded in 1823 by Revd George Young. Before this, the museum was located on Pier Road where the Quayside restaurant now stands. This was the building where Bram Stoker 'discovered' the real Dracula.

By the end of the nineteenth century the museum on Pier Road was in a state of disrepair and plans were drawn to move, but nothing happened until 1920 when the death of a solicitor, Robert Elliott Pannett, led to a park with a museum being established under the terms of his will. This was achieved by 1931.

The museum contains the Pannett Collection, but is particularly strong in fossils, relics from Captain Cook's voyages, and the mysterious Hand of Glory. The museum is open to the public from 9-30am to 4-30pm throughout the year except Mondays, but is always best to check on opening times.

See also: Fossils, Hand of Glory, Pannett Park

N

North York Moors Historical Railway Trust

The North York Moors Historic Railway (NYMHR), which is steam operated, is one of the glories of North Yorkshire. The railway is run by a trust and is 18 miles in length. The line links Pickering, Levisham, Newton Dale, Goathland and Grosmont, but trains can get to Whitby over lines that are owned by Network Rail. Although much of the line was closed in 1965, the NYMHR opened from Pickering to Grosmont in 1973 and from there to Whitby in 2007. The line is a great tourist attraction and, of its kind, perhaps the most successful in Britain.

O

Old Town Hall

Whitby's Old Town Hall is described as being in Crossgate, though that street is not listed in the current street directory of the town. A better description of its site would be that the building is in the Market Place, or, perhaps, on Church Street or Sandgate. The building is often known as 'The Cross' because the Market Cross was sited there.

In the past there was a Town Hall on the western banks of the Esk but, in 1788, the Town Hall was moved to its present location in the Old Town, to the east of the river.

Below left: Whitby Old Town Hall on the east side of town. It also served as a courtroom and a meeting room.

Below right: There is still a market held at the Old Town Hall on Whitby's east side.

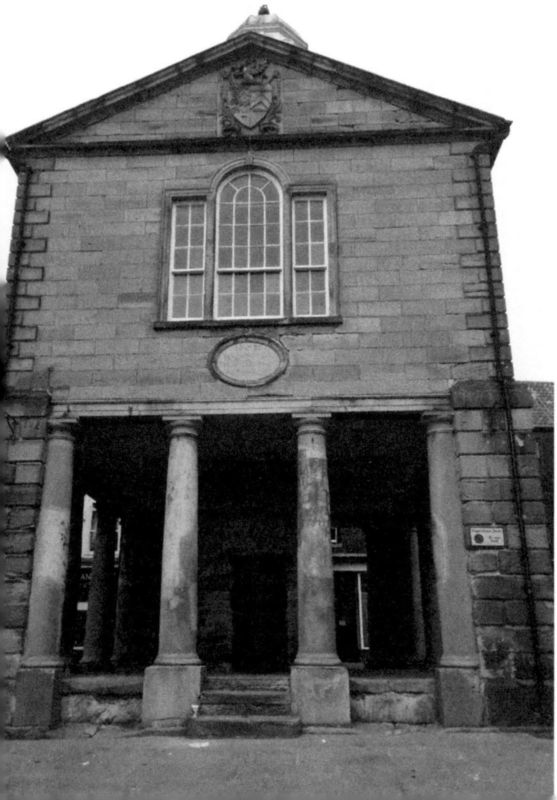

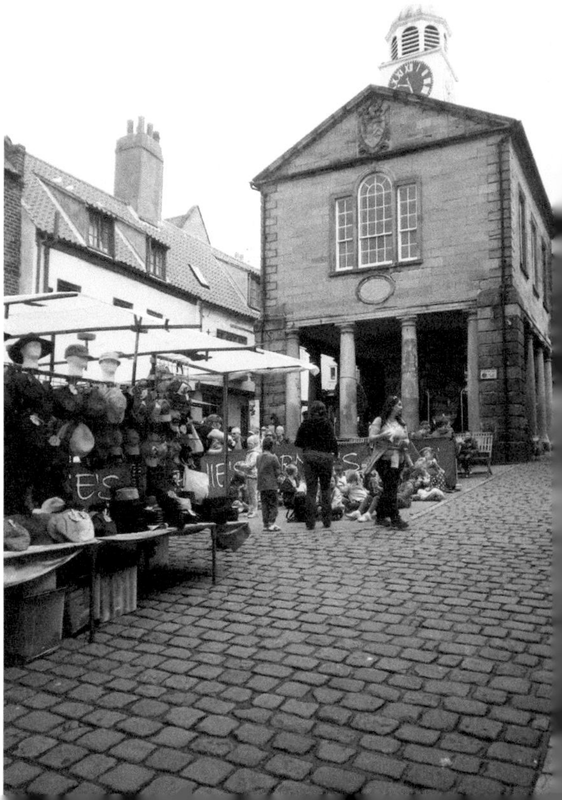

The site was formerly occupied by a Tollbooth, which had become dilapidated and was deemed, in the opinion of Nathaniel Cholmley, the Lord of the Manor, who footed the bill for the new building, to be 'unworthy of the improvement of Whitby'.

The building served as a town hall, a market place, a courtroom and a meeting place. The upper floor is supported by Tuscan pillars and there is a fine clock tower, which was paid for by the people of Whitby.

As a meeting place, the building, in 1823, hosted the first meeting of the Whitby Literary and Philosophical Society whose early aims included the finding of a space in which to display fossils found in the Whitby area. These are now on display at Pannett Park.

With regard to the building's use as a court, several different courts have been held in there, including the Court Leet, and the Court of Piepowders. Whitby's stocks were conveniently located nearby.

See also: Piepowders, Court of

Order of the Holy Paraclete

The Order of the Holy Paraclete is an order of religious nuns who have their Mother House, St Hilda's Priory, at Sneaton Castle, 2 miles south of Whitby. The order's name is translated as 'comforter' but the words 'helper, consoler and advocate' are equally applicable. Work began at Sneaton in 1915, where the order has its offices, but the nuns can be called to serve in other areas. The first of these was at Tonge Moor, in Lancashire, in 1924, where they worked for four years in a local school. At the present time, the order has branch houses at Bishopthorpe, in Yorkshire; Dormantown, in Middlesborough; Sleights, in Yorkshire; and at York. There are also two branch houses abroad.

P

Pannett Park

In 1920, Robert Elliott Pannett died and in his will he gave up land that he owned in Whitby to be turned into a park where the people of Whitby could enjoy fresh air, trees and flowers – away from the sea winds, the cliffs and the beach. Pannett had bought the land in 1902 and it had mainly been used for orchards and market gardens.

Below left: Pannett Park is a little piece of idyllic countryside in the middle of a busy fishing town.

Below right: Hidden away in the midst of Pannett Park is the lily pool. Well worth seeking out on a summer's day.

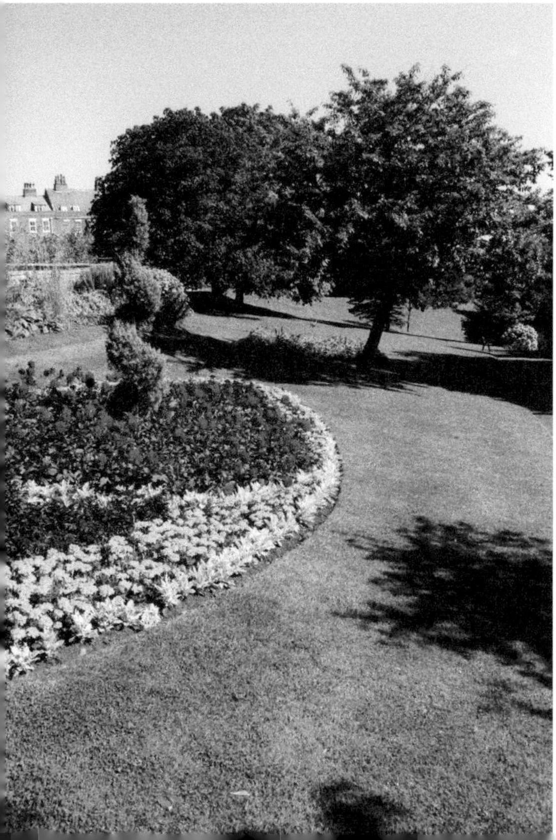

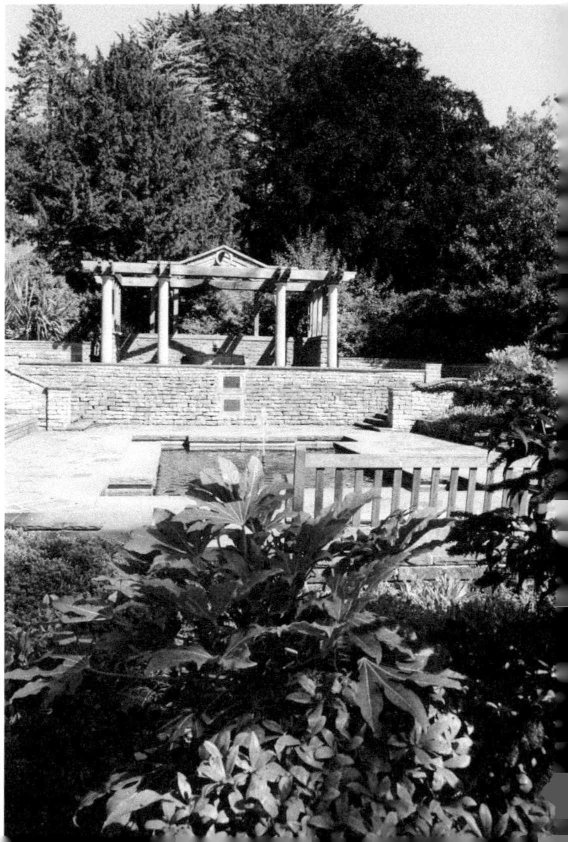

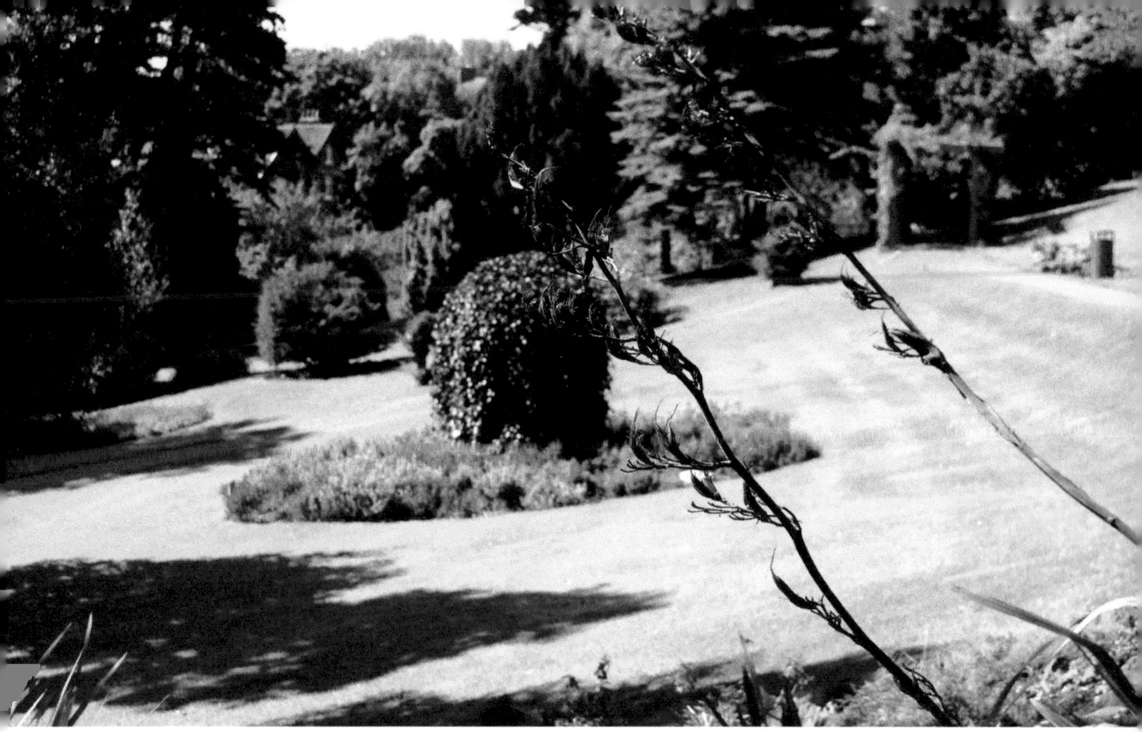

The well-kept gardens of the park are a great place to relax.

He had tried to persuade the council, on several occasions, to turn the property into a public park, but to no avail.

Pannett had set up a trust that ensured that, upon his death, the park would become a reality. The plans included the construction of an art gallery where the public could view his collection. In 1931 this was extended to include the collection of Whitby Museum. The park was designed by a firm of landscape designers from Darlington and construction for the art gallery began in 1927.

Today the park is a peaceful and beautiful place to visit with small gardens hidden away. Some of these small gardens reflect Whitby's past, such as the Jurassic Garden and the South Seas Garden, and there is a large ornate pond waiting to be discovered amongst the carefully maintained shrubs and trees.

See also: Museum

Pantiles

A pantile is a roofing tile that has a cross-section in an ogee curve (shaped like an S) with one curve longer than the other. The tiles are shaped to overlap the next and are made from fired clay.

Pantiles are very commonly used in buildings in the English coastal towns of the east coast. They were first imported from Holland in the seventeenth century. Roofs made from pantiles are lighter than flat-tile equivalents and roofs made with this material can be laid at a lower pitch. In Whitby many roofs are made from pantiles, giving the town a very distinctive red appearance.

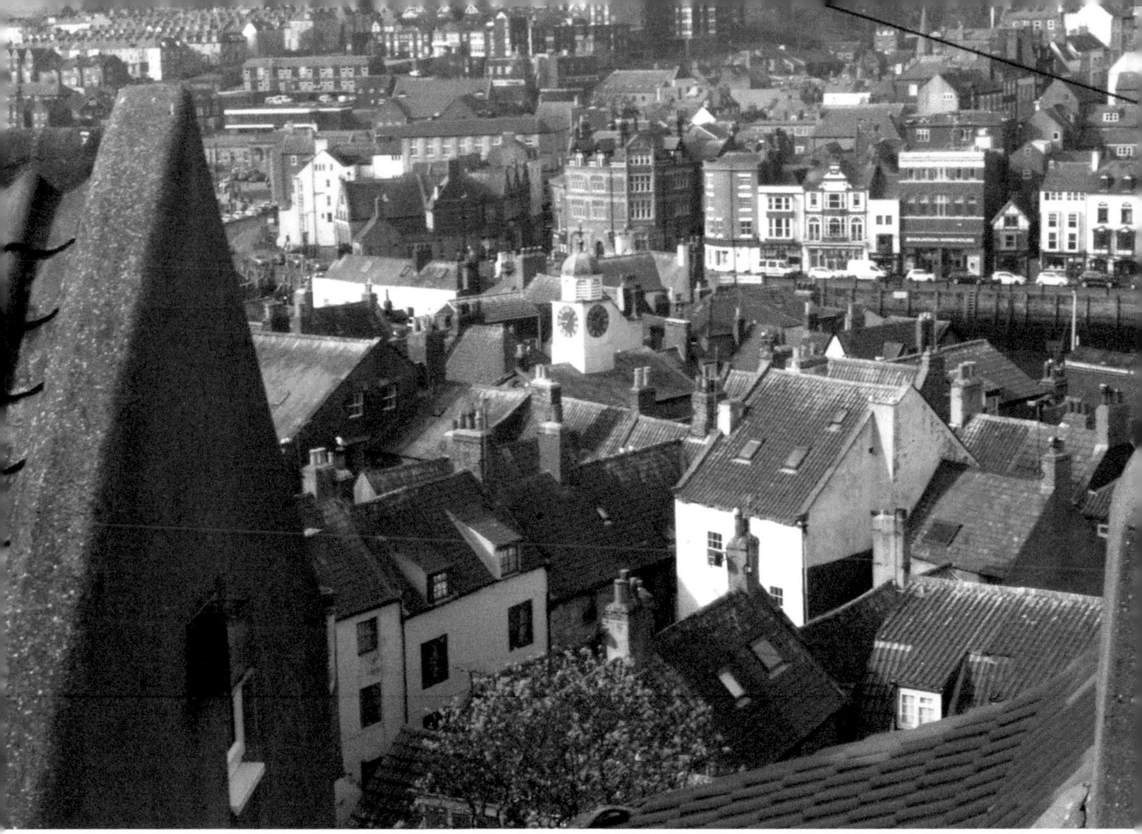

The red pantiles of Whitby's rooftops are an iconic site.

Pavilion

The Pavilion was built in 1878 as a proscenium arch-style theatre (meaning that an ornate arch marked the line between the stage and the audience). The Pavilion can seat 380 people and the stalls can be removed to form a dance floor, making the building quite versatile. Today it serves as a cinema, concert hall, theatre, exhibition centre, and even a specialist market hall for antiques or Goth articles. The Pavilion also has a café where refreshments may be taken whilst admiring the views of the coast.

Piepowders, Court of

In the Middle Ages many towns and villages had Courts of Piepowders. They were set up to regulate market and itinerant traders. The word comes from the French '*piets poudres*', the people with dusty feet, or travellers.

Cases were held in such courts by local men, who could also try those who were suspected of small offences. The courts were well regulated and evidence-based, both sides having the opportunity to address the court.

It is likely that Whitby had a Court of Piepowders in the Middle Ages, and it is known that one still operated in the eighteenth century when the Old Town Hall was built.

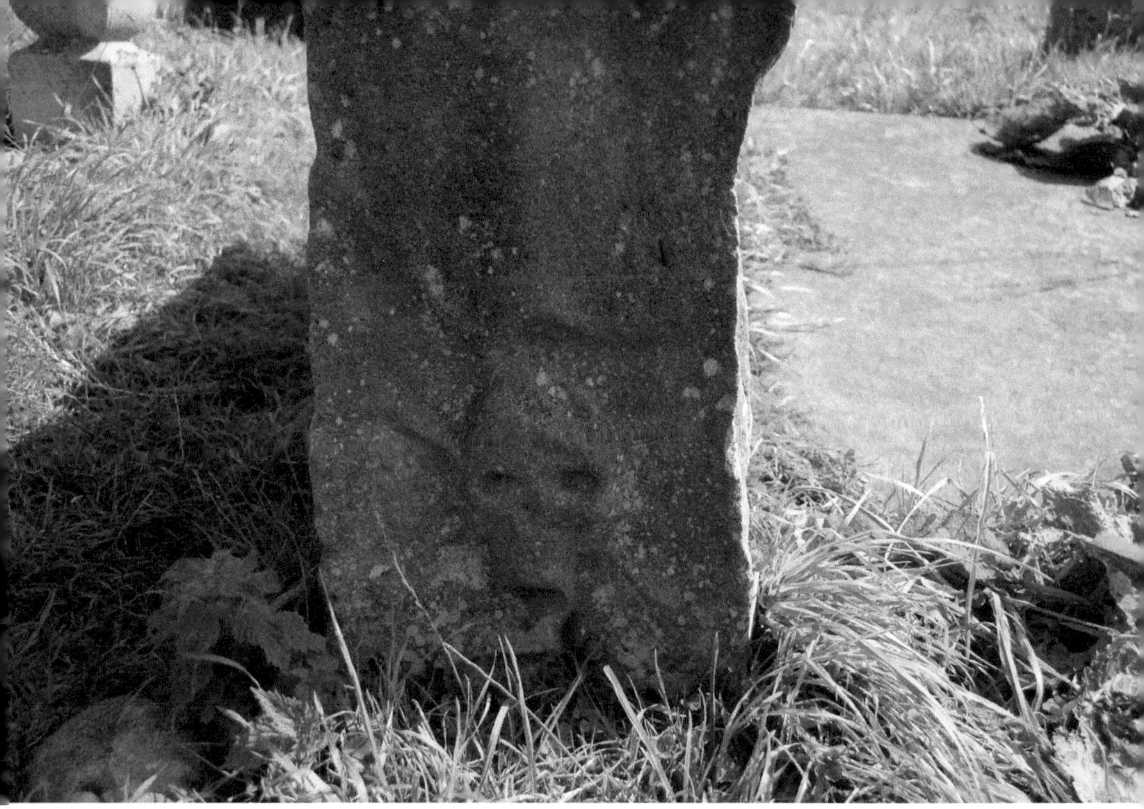

Do these skull and crossbones mark the site of a pirate's grave? Or is it a warning that this is the last resting place of Dracula?

Pirates' Graves

St Mary's churchyard is the location of two graves with gruesome decoration; each has a very distinct skull and crossbones design, which has led to them being dubbed the Pirates' Graves. It has been speculated that these graves might have been the resting place of the vampire Dracula when he landed at Whitby, or even that they are the graves of master masons who used the Skull of Sidon in their imagery, or even a Knight Templar. The actual truth behind these graves is that it was once a common practice to carve such imagery into a gravestone as a reminder of man's mortality and nothing more sinister.

See also: Graveyard

Polar Bear

Opposite the Dolphin Inn, if you look just a little higher than eye level, you will spot a rather curious character keeping watch over the harbour. This polar bear, Snow Prince, has been stood in this location for years and is actually a Christmas decoration that has been allowed to remain. However, the presence of a polar bear in Whitby is nothing new.

During the whaling years, polar bears were often captured as they could command a great deal of money for furs or even as live exhibits in zoos. The easiest ways to capture a polar bear would be to either throw a noose around one when it was swimming, and then store it in a cage, or, rather more heartless, was to take a bear cub after shooting its mother.

This is what is reported to have happened when Captain William Scoresby obtained a polar bear on his return from whaling in the Greenland waters. He successfully tamed the bear and it lived, in chains, under Spital Bridge in Whitby, where it was fed on seagulls and fish.

The bear became something of a local attraction and was teased by the townsfolk to the point where, enraged, it broke free and escaped into Cock Mill Woods. Armed men went after the bear and cornered it, but before it could be shot, Scoresby, with a piece of rope, walked up to the bear, patted the animal and slipped the rope around its neck. The bear, recognising its master, became quiet and allowed itself to be led away.

What happened to the bear after this is not fully known. Some reports say that it was sent to London Zoo and others say that it died in captivity in Whitby, its bones lost in the Esk. But what we do know is that Snow Prince is likely to stay where he is for a very long time.

See also: Scoresby, Whaling

Prospect of Whitby

Though not in Whitby, a few words about this famous public house in Wapping, in East London, will not go amiss. The Prospect of Whitby is a Grade II listed building on the banks of the Thames. It probably dates from the 1520s but it could be older. Initially, it was known as 'The Devil's Tavern', because of its associations with riverside ruffians, robbers and smugglers, and not, as you might think, because it had any connections with Whitby.

The building was reconstructed after a fire in the eighteenth century, and refaced in yellow brick in the nineteenth, but, inside, the flagged floors, for example, are thought to be original.

The present name was applied when a ship called *The Prospect* was moored in the Thames, close to the public house. The ship, which had been registered in Whitby, became a landmark and the name of the pub changed to the Prospect of Whitby to reflect this.

The pub was a favourite haunt of a few well-known men including the diarist Samuel Pepys, the infamous Judge Jeffries, the artists David Cox, Turner and Whistler and the author Charles Dickens. Of these, Dickens certainly visited Whitby.

Q

Queen Victoria

In 1861 Queen Victoria's life was shattered by the death of her beloved husband, Prince Albert, and, amid her personal tragedy, she unwittingly became a patron of one of Whitby's most famous industries.

Wearing mourning dress for the next forty years of her life, Queen Victoria required jewellery to match her sombre clothes and the black gemstone jet was the ideal choice. Although jet was found across the world, it was manufactured into jewellery in Whitby and, before long, Queen Victoria had made jet the only jewellery that was permitted to be worn at court.

From the Queen's adoption of jet jewellery, John Storr and W. Hamond were able to increase their sales and become leaders in the sale of Whitby Jet.

See also: Jet

R

Railways

Railways came to Whitby very early but, initially, they were not steam powered. The first line was, however, an immediate success, carrying 10,000 tons of stone and many passengers to the town in the first year. The line was opened in 1836 and was built by the Whitby & Pickering Railway. It was a single-track horse-hauled railway. George Stephenson was the engineer.

In 1845, the W&P was taken over by the York & North Midland Railway, which converted the track to double and introduced steam locomotives. It was this company that built the present impressive station in Whitby. Nine years later, the Y&NM became part of the North Eastern Railway, which built the Esk Valley line. This was opened to a junction at Grosmont in 1865.

Two other lines served Whitby first: in 1883, from Loftus to the north of Whitby, and, secondly, from Scarborough in 1885. This made four lines serving the town.

The NER became part of the L&NER in 1923 and this became British Railways on nationalisation in 1948. The Beeching Report of 1963 recommended the closure of all railways surviving in Whitby. The line to the north had been closed in 1958 and, of the remaining three, only the Esk line to Middlesbrough survived.

Today, Whitby is most well-known for its association with the North York Moors Railway.

See also: North York Moors Historical Railway Trust

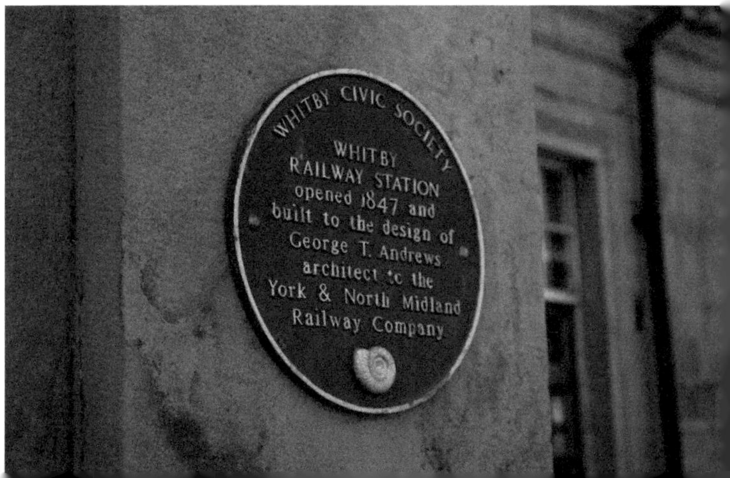

A Whitby Civic Society plaque commemorates the opening of Whitby train station.

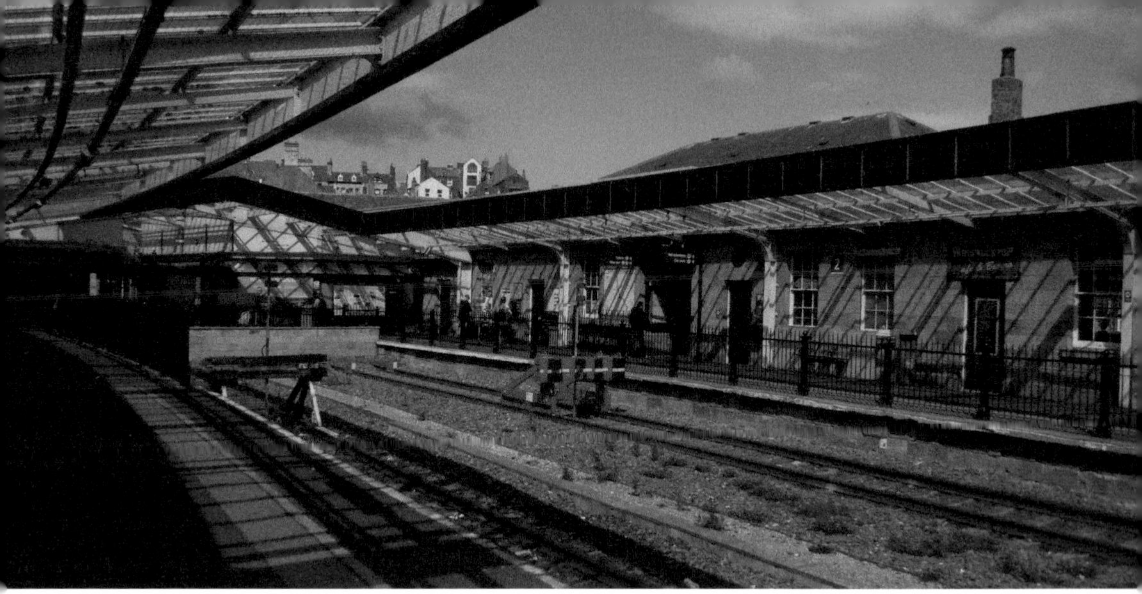

The end of the line! This is where thousands of tourists would have disembarked, having arrived at Whitby for their holidays.

Regatta

For a few days in August Whitby harbour comes alive, when maritime entertainment and competition are the order of the day. This has been taking place for 170 years. Arguably one of Whitby's biggest events, the Whitby Regatta features races by both sailing and rowing boats, a display by the Royal Air Force's Red Arrows, and finishes with a spectacular firework display.

The Whitby Regatta started with fishermen competing against each other in their small boats. In 1847 the Royal Yorkshire Yacht Club hosted the 'Whitby Challenge Cup' and, from then until the 1930s, yacht racing was a big feature of the regatta, although rowing had become more competitive with rowing clubs forming. Today the Scarborough Amateur Rowing Club, the Friendship Rowing Club, and the Whitby Fisherman's Amateur Rowing Club still compete in the regatta.

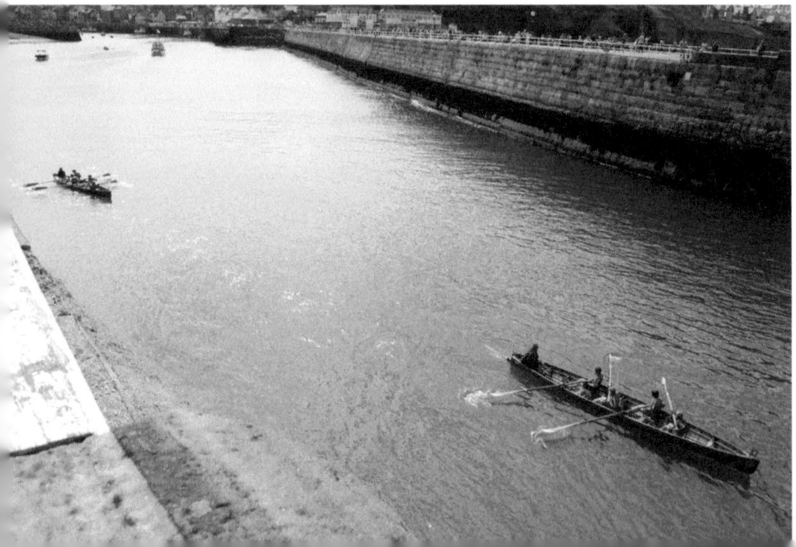

Getting some practice in. A rowing team prepare for the annual race at the Whitby Regatta.

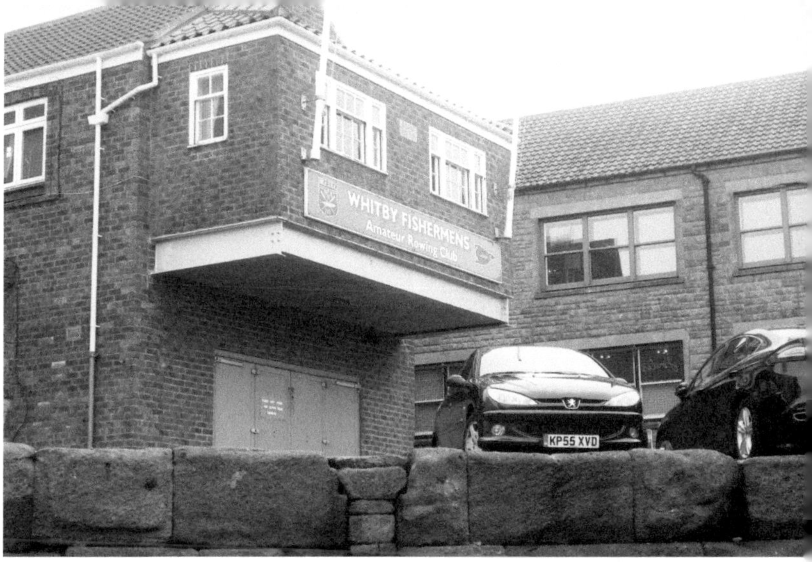

One of the Whitby rowing clubs. The regatta is the highlight of the year for these clubs.

Resolution

HMS *Resolution* was a Royal Navy sloop in which James Cook made his second and third voyages. The vessel was launched in 1770 and was a North Sea collier, originally named the *Marquis of Granby*, which had been built in Whitby by Fishburn's. It was bought by the Royal Navy in 1771 for £4,151 and renamed HMS *Drake*, but not to upset the Spanish, the name of HMS *Resolution* was adopted.

Cook was in command when HMS *Resolution* set off from Plymouth in July 1772. Its mission was to sail to the Antarctic, where, in 1773, it became the first ship to sail across the Antarctic Circle, a feat which the *Resolution* achieved on two more occasions. On this voyage Cook disproved Alexander Dalrymple's theory of a super southern continent.

HMS *Resolution* returned to England in 1775 and was decommissioned. Cook had said that it was 'the ship of my choice' and that it was 'the fittest for service of any I have seen', so it was brought back into the Royal Navy fold for Cook's third and final voyage. This included a visit to the Arctic where the Circle was crossed in 1778. It was crossed again under the command of Charles Clerke after the untimely death of Cook in 1779. The ship returned to England in 1780 and was converted into a transport vessel a year later and sent to the West Indies. By that time the American War of Independence had broken out and the ship was captured, in 1782, by the French, the allies of the Americans. It was lost at sea, under French command, in the same year.

Royal Crescent

The Royal Crescent was the idea of George Hudson, who saw the opportunity, at Whitby, to emulate places like Bath. He created the Khyber Pass to make it easier to handle the building materials brought to the site. The Crescent, with fantastic sea views and a floral garden, would be the highlight of the West Cliff.

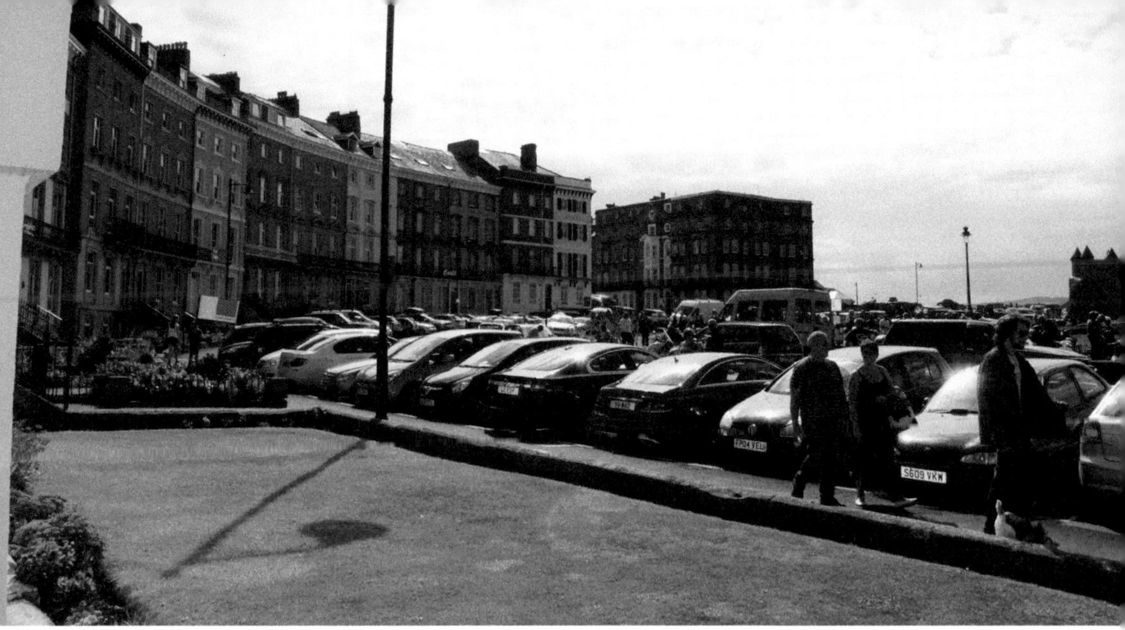

The Royal Crescent – at least half of it. It remains incomplete due to the bankruptcy of its designer.

However, the Royal Crescent remains unfinished. Hudson had grand ideas that were also expensive; he simply ran out of money before his project could be completed. Today, Royal Crescent is a mix of private homes, guest houses, and hotels; one of the guest houses was where Bram Stoker would stay when writing *Dracula*. His room can be hired today.

See also: Hudson, George; Khyber Pass

Ruswarp

Ruswarp is a village in the Esk valley, west of Whitby. Ruswarp used to be spelled Risewarp, from the Old English 'hris wearp', which means 'the silted land overgrown with brushwood'. The village has an iron bridge, and a tall brick viaduct (of 5,250,000 bricks). The latter carries the Cinder Track, a walk and cycle way, which is owned by the transport charity Sustrans.

The older houses can be found at the foot of a steep hill where a modern church, St Bartholomew's, is located. Its tower is 120 feet high and, inside, is a bullet-scarred crucifix picked up on the battlefields of Ypres. Near the church is Old Hall, which was the home of Captain Bushell who, during the Civil War of the seventeenth century, could not decide whether he was for the King or for Parliament. It was he who betrayed Scarborough Castle to the Royalists, for which he paid with his life.

The River Esk used to power several corn mills in the village but the last of them closed in 1962. However, the Ruswarp Hydro, which opened in 2012, generates electricity, taking its water from an old mill scheme. Ruswarp's attractions include pleasure boats which allow visitors to discover the River Esk, the only river in Yorkshire that has migratory salmon.

S

Sandsend

Sandsend is an attractive, small coastal village north of Whitby. Its origins go back to the days when alum was mined in the area, though there has long since been a small fishing industry based in the village.

Sandsend and East Row were once separate villages, both dependent on alum mining. The Redcar & Middlesbrough Union Railway was constructed to serve the villages in 1883 but it closed before the Beeching Report in 1958.

Gradually the villages grew together and now they have a small share in the local tourist industry. There are a few quaint fishermen's cottages. Sandsend has a very attractive beach and there are grassy cliffs at the base where there are rock pools much loved by children. The villages have a post office, a pub (the Hart Inn), a church and a tennis club and fossils are found regularly on the beach.

The abandoned alum mines make an interesting local walk and are part of The Sandsend Trail, which has been described as having Hobbit-style landscapes, a moon-like terrain, an old abandoned railway tunnel and a shipwreck. Mulgrave Castle, a Norman ruin at Lythe, is nearby. In Lythe, St Oswald's Church has Anglo-Scandinavian stones.

Scampi

It has been claimed that Whitby is the home of scampi. There is certainly a Whitby-based firm which markets Whitby Scampi and this product can be bought for home consumption and eaten in restaurants all over the country.

Scampi is also known as the Dublin Bay Prawn, or the Norway Lobster. It is an edible lobster, though monkfish tails have been used and sold in Britain, illegally, as scampi. The scampi lobster is of the order of 'Decapoda' class crustacea, which is widespread in the Mediterranean and the north-eastern Atlantic from Africa to Norway and Iceland.

Until recently scampi was one of the lesser-used fish in restaurants and cafés, but it has been championed as a sustainable source of protein. Scampi is usually fried

in breadcrumbs and served with potato chips and peas. In the United States there is a National Scampi Day – the 29 April.
See also: Fishing

Scoresby, William (Junior)

William Scoresby was born in 1789. He was the son of William Scoresby, who had earned himself a fortune as a whaler. At the age of eleven he made his first voyage with his father and, at the age of thirteen, William became his father's apprentice. By sixteen, he was first mate and then, at twenty-one, captain of his father's vessel, the *Resolution*.

From 1806, William attended natural philosophy and chemistry classes at Edinburgh University. This coincided with the beginnings of his observations about science. He continued with whaling but published about meteorology, the natural history of the polar regions and made observations about snow and crystals.

In 1813, William made it known that the Arctic Ocean has a warmer temperature at considerable depths. Three years later he was in command of the ship *Esk*, which had been damaged by ice and was threatening to sink. William surrendered most of his catch and, with the help of his brother-in-law on board accompanying ship the *John*, the Esk was repaired, saving the lives his crew.

He was elected a Fellow of the Royal Society of Edinburgh in 1819, and he published a paper, 'On the anomaly in the Variation of the Magnetic Needle'. This was part of his aim to improve the reliability of ship's compasses, part of the solution being the invention of new grades of steel. Three years later, he surveyed the Greenland coast and, at the same time, undertook his last whaling voyage.

On his return to England he learned of the death of his wife and he turned his attention to the Church. It was at this time that William published, in Edinburgh, his most influential work, *The Journal of a Voyage to the Northern Whale Fishery*.

Having left whaling, which was now in decline, William undertook Divinity studies at Cambridge. He was ordained and appointed, successively, to churches at Bessingby (Yorkshire), Liverpool, Exeter and Bradford. This latter appointment was as vicar in 1839, where he stayed until 1847. His clerical life did not prevent him from the furtherance of science. He was, for example, much involved in making scientific topics more available to the public and he worked with James Joule on electromagnetism and optics.

At Bradford, William found that its working people were suffering from many social problems. He became associated with the campaign to improve factory and living conditions and he founded the first Church day schools in Bradford. William Scoresby died at Torquay on 21 March 1857. A blue plaque in his memory can be found at Bradford Cathedral.

Scoresby, William (Senior)

William Scoresby (1760–1829) was born near Pickering, the son of a farmer. As a young man he was an agricultural labourer, but he went to sea in 1785, joining the whaling ship the *Henrietta*. William proved his worth at sea and was captain of the ship by 1791.

He was very successful, bringing large catches of whales back to Whitby for processing. His share of the catch made him very wealthy, but it was not this that made him famous. He invented the Crow's Nest, an example of which can be seen in Whitby Museum. The Crow's Nest was to provide shelter for ship's navigators who did their work at the top of the main mast.

He also suggested the use of sledges to reach the North Pole and, in 1806, father and son on the same ship, he sailed to latitude 81 degrees 30 north, which broke the British record for sailing the furthest north. He retired from whaling, along with his son, in 1823.

Shipbuilding

Given its coastal location and the seafaring occupations of its residents, there has always been an element of ship and boat building in Whitby, but, by the end of the eighteenth century, the town had become one of the most important shipbuilding centres in the country. In 1700 there were 113 ships registered to Whitby shipowners, but in 1776 that figure had risen to 251. In 1730 the harbour was enlarged to take bigger ships and, within years, the alum, fishing, whaling and coal-carrying industries were growing rapidly. This resulted in existing ships requiring more maintenance and the demand for vessels themselves increased.

Regular shipbuilding yards were established in the harbour. The earliest was that of Jarvis Coates, who died in 1739. Ten years later his son, also known as Jarvis, started his own yard, and, in 1760, James Simpson did likewise. The yards of Coates (junior) was taken over by Fishburn & Broderick, one of the best known in Whitby, and that of Simpson, by William Hustler, who later sold to Messrs Longborne.

In the 1770s, Whitby was given a great boost when James Cook chose Whitby ships for his voyages of discovery. When his choice of the ship, *Resolution*, was challenged, Cook commented, 'I can assure you, I have never set foot in a finer ship.' This was in response to Lloyd's of London who believed the vessels made in London, at the time the most important shipbuilding centre, were much superior to those made in the provinces.

Between 1776 and 1783, Whitby made an average of twenty or twenty-one ships per year. By 1792–1806, this had risen to twenty-four or twenty-five ships. In 1802, thirty-nine ships were built, but, by 1807–16 the average had fallen to only fourteen ships. In the latter year, 1816, Whitby owners possessed 280 vessels in all categories.

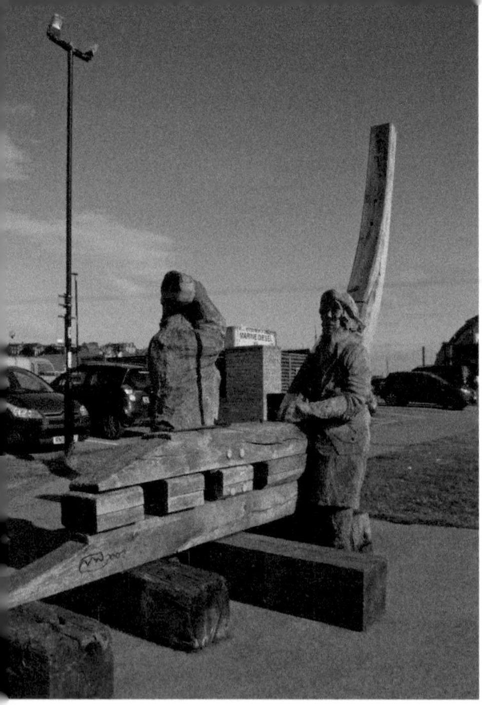

Left: This memorial at the marina commemorates the Whitby shipbuilding industry, which was vital to the town in years gone by.

Below: Shipbuilding continues in Whitby. The town built many ships, including all four of Captain Cook's vessels.

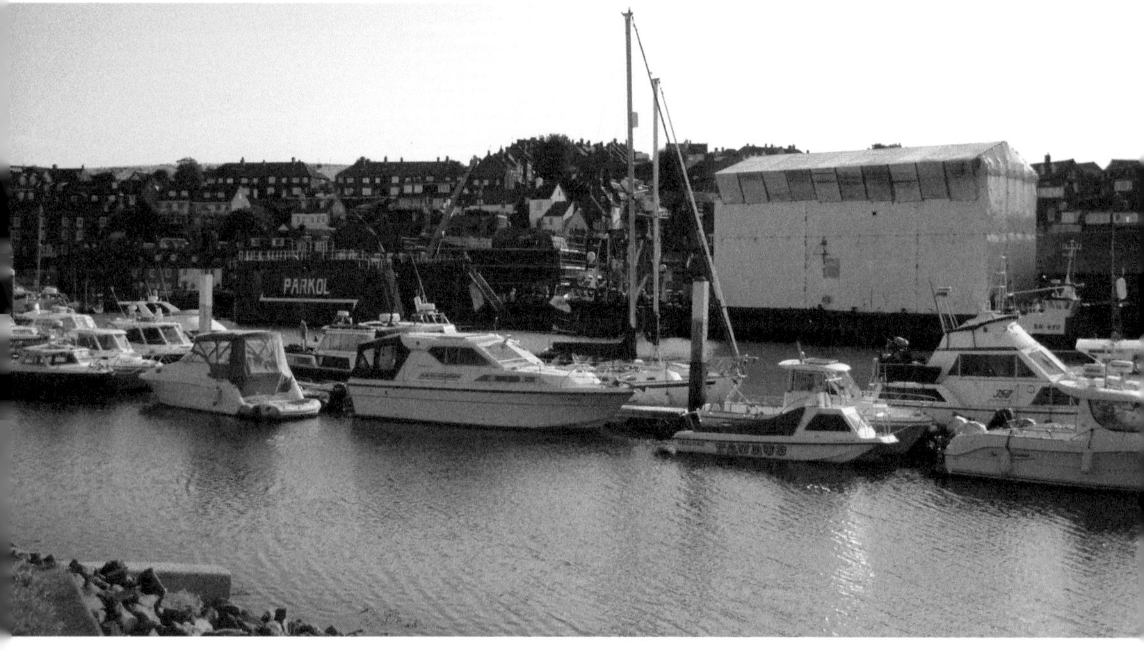

Collectively, their tonnage was 46,341 (an average of 165.5 tons) and there were 2,674 registered seamen in the town. New yards were opened; at one stage there were eleven shipbuilders operating in Whitby.

By the end of the first quarter of the nineteenth century, the best years of Whitby shipbuilding were behind the town. The industry continued to flourish further to the north-east in Tyneside, Wearside and Teesside, where larger vessels, incorporating steam, could be made from iron rather that the wooden sailing vessels of Whitby.

Sneaton (and Sneaton Castle)

Sneaton (Snetune in the Domesday Book of 1086) is 2 miles south of Whitby. The place name means 'the tun (or fence or enclosure) by woodland' and was within the Yorkshire holdings of Hugh Lupus, Earl of Chester, at the time of Domesday. The village has several interesting buildings including Sneaton Castle and Rigg Mill, which has an old waterwheel. There are three waterfalls near the latter.

There is a church, of ancient foundation, dedicated to St Hilda, and this contains a font of 1108. In 1138, the church was dependent on the refounded Whitby Abbey. The present church is understood to have been the third built on the site. It was built by James Wilson, of Sneaton Castle, in 1823.

James Wilson was born in Corrie, in Annandale, in the County of Dumfries, in Scotland. He made his fortune as a slave owner at the Cane Grove Plantation in St Vincent, one of the Windward Islands in the West Indies. In 1827 Wilson employed 231 slaves at Cane Grove where be built a hospital for them. He returned to Britain, buying the Sneaton Manor estate, near Whitby, in 1820, when he started to build Sneaton Castle. Wilson later became the MP for York and, at his death in 1830, he was a Lt-colonel of militia of the isle of St Vincent and deputy lieutenant for the county of Yorkshire. Today, Sneaton Castle is shared by the Sneaton Castle Centre and the Order of the Holy Paraclete, an order of nuns.

See also: Order of the Holy Paraclete

Spital Bridge

Spital Bridge is the continuation of Church Street to the south. The word comes from the Middle English 'spitel', a place of rest and/or recovery (from illness).

Close to the bridge stood the Hospital of St John, one of two such institutions in Whitby. It was founded in 1109 by William de Percy, abbot of Whitby, for a single person suffering from leprosy. The endowment was augmented, and the hospital was enlarged to take in a small number of poor persons. None of the building remains above ground but, below ground, some of the building survives.

Steps, 199

One of the most iconic of Whitby's landmarks can be found on the East Cliff, just below St Mary's Church. It is a sweeping staircase that takes those who use it from the town to the churchyard. Despite the climb, the views along the way are some of the most rewarding to be found in the town. The steps are first mentioned in 1340 when they were made of wood! The stone steps that exist today are a relatively new creation having been constructed in 1774.

There are what appears to be a number of benches on the steps, but they were not built to sit and rest. They were for coffins to rest on as they were carried up to the graveyard, allowing the pall-bearers time to catch their breath.

Tradition dictates that first-time users of the steps should count them to see if there are actually 199. There have been many differences of opinion. John Wesley, for instance claimed only 191. Today most people count either 198 or 200.

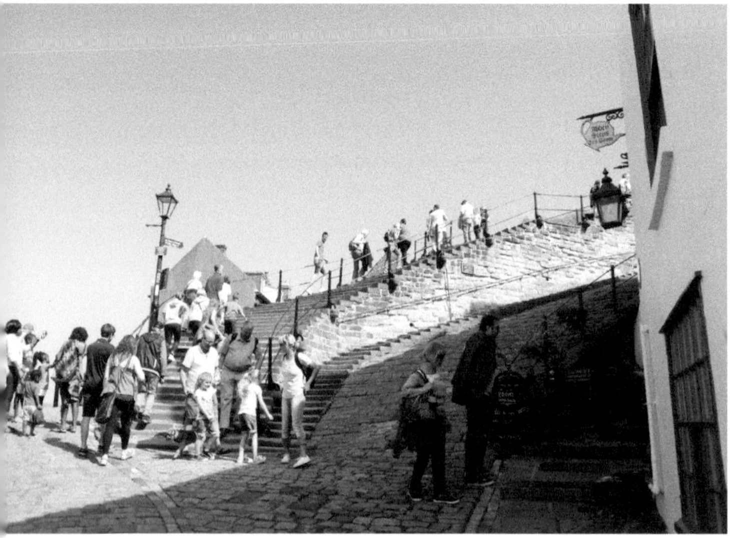

Left: It is almost a rite de passage in Whitby to make your way up the 199 Steps. Don't forget to count them carefully!

Below: The views from the 199 Steps are stunning, whatever the time of day. The physical effort of climbing the steps is forgotten when you see the outstanding view.

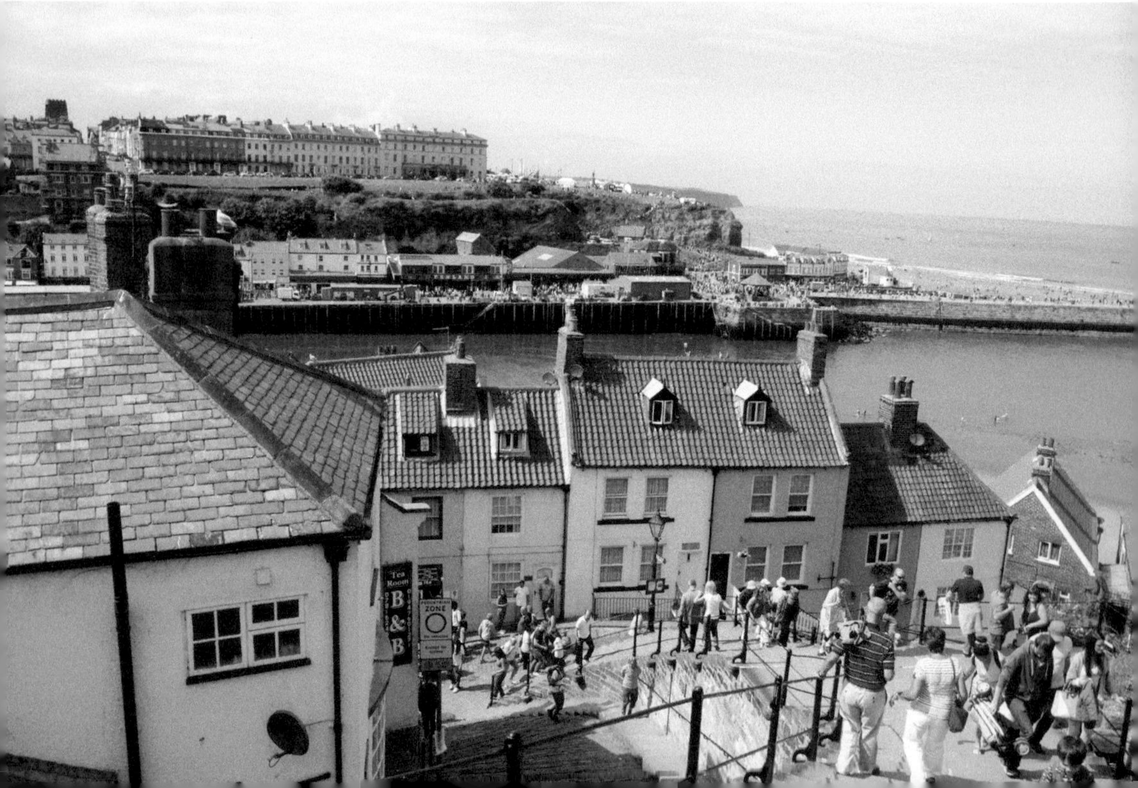

St Mary's Church

St Mary's, the parish church of Whitby, has stood on the East Cliff from around 1110. It is Grade I listed. The building is located close to the ruins of Whitby Abbey and overlooks the town.

It has been suggested that the church was the original conventual church of the Norman refoundation of Whitby Abbey and that it was built by Abbot William de Percy. However, the building was presented to the people of the town for use as parish church, when the monastic church was completed. The building is not recorded in the Domesday Book, but it is mentioned in a late twelfth-century charter.

Though encompassing several different architectural styles – Norman, Gothic and Georgian – a few traces of the Norman church remain, particularly the chancel arch, which is hidden by a more recent gallery. In addition, there are some round-headed windows, which are typical of Norman architecture.

There are several church guides which tell more of the architecture of the building, but worthy of note are the squat tower, which has an embattled parapet and dates to the sixteenth century. There are eight bells, six of which are eighteenth century and the other two of the mid-nineteenth century.

Inside, the church is unlike any religious church you will have ever seen. It has been described as a 'riot' of box pews, galleries and pillars, too many of all of them, some

St Mary's Church at the top of the 199 Steps. You will seldom find such a majestic and beautiful church in the country.

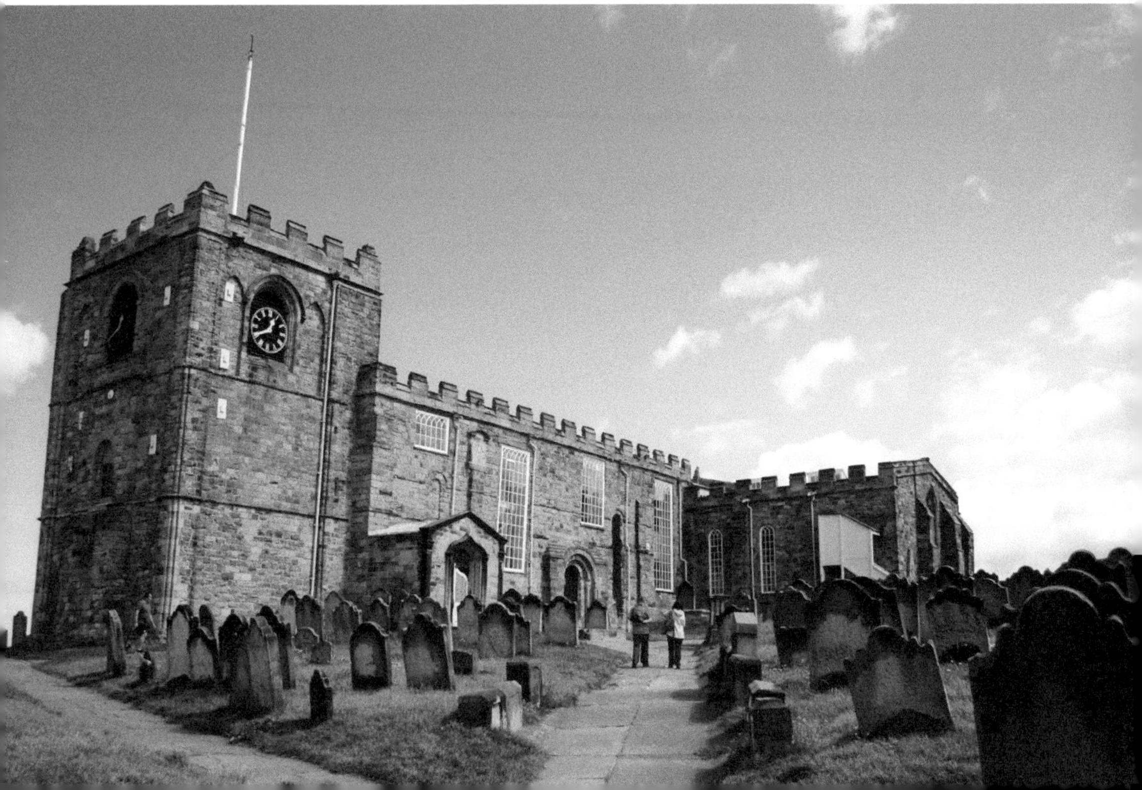

getting in the way of each other. Much of this work dates to the eighteenth century and it was carried out by men more used to building ships than churches.

St Mary's is a rare example of a church interior completely untouched by Victorian restoration. It might look to be unplanned, which it is, but the large eighteenth-century windows flood the building with light. There is a very large, almost incongruous three-decker pulpit from 1748, the only three-decker in the world standing in the middle of a church.

Stoker, Bram

In 1890 the Irish author Bram Stoker was holidaying in Whitby with his family. He had already started on a story about a bloodsucking monster that he called Count Wampyr, but all that was soon to change.

Stoker would walk around the town listening to tales of ghosts and local legends. He learned of a Russian schooner, the *Dmitry*, which, a few years before, had run aground on the beach at Tate Hill (just below the East Cliff). Then he visited the Whitby Public Lending Library and read about Wallachia and Moldovia, where he learnt about a fierce tyrant who impaled his foes on wooden stakes. This was Vlad Tepes, also known as Vlad the Impaler, and known by his people as Dracula.

Stoker began to weave the local legends into the story he was writing. Dracula, for instance, arrived in Whitby on board a wrecked Russian schooner, the *Demeter*, that would run aground on Tate Hill Sands. Dracula leapt from the wrecked ship, taking the form of a great black dog. There is a Whitby (and North Yorkshire) legend of a fierce black dog that haunts the streets at night.

Much of the Whitby sections of the novel show how much of the local character Stoker wove into the story and it is still possible to visit many of the locations in the novel. It is

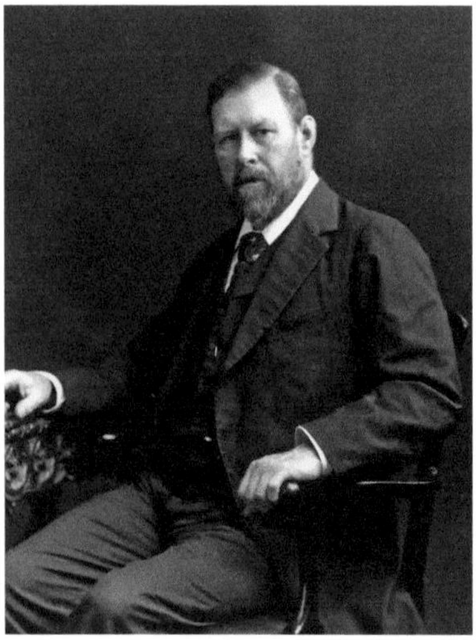

Whitby's most famous holidaymaker? Bram Stoker – the Irish author who set scenes in *Dracula* after visiting Whitby.

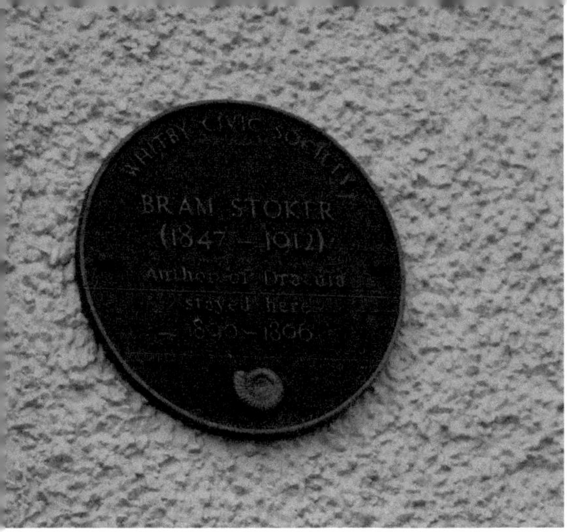

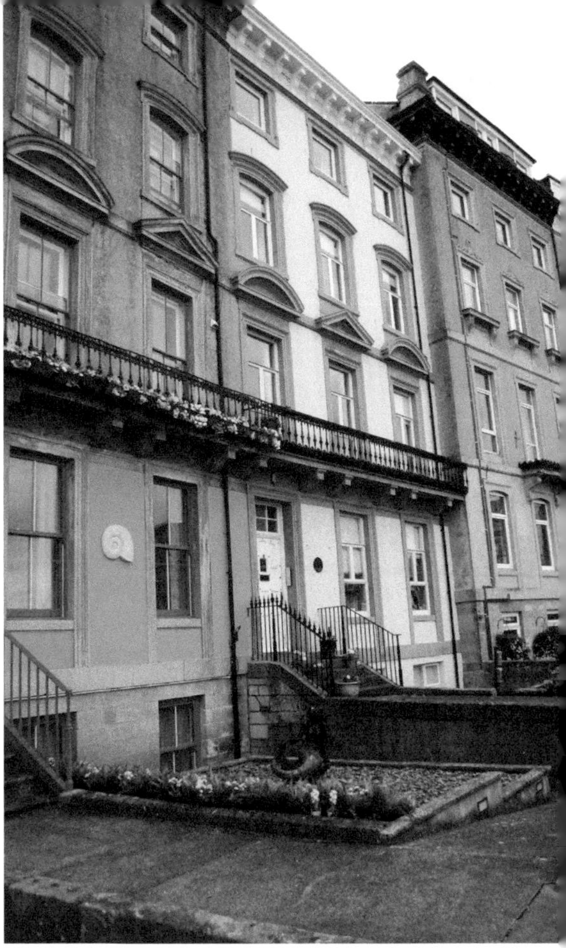

Above: A civic society plaque leaves you in no doubt that this is where *Dracula* author Bram Stoker stayed.

Right: The narrow guest house on Royal Crescent where Bram Stoker stayed when visiting Whitby. It is hard to believe that the world's most famous vampire was created here.

Below: A bench in the memory of Bram Stoker sits on Spion Kop with views across the harbour. The view will have changed little since Stoker's day.

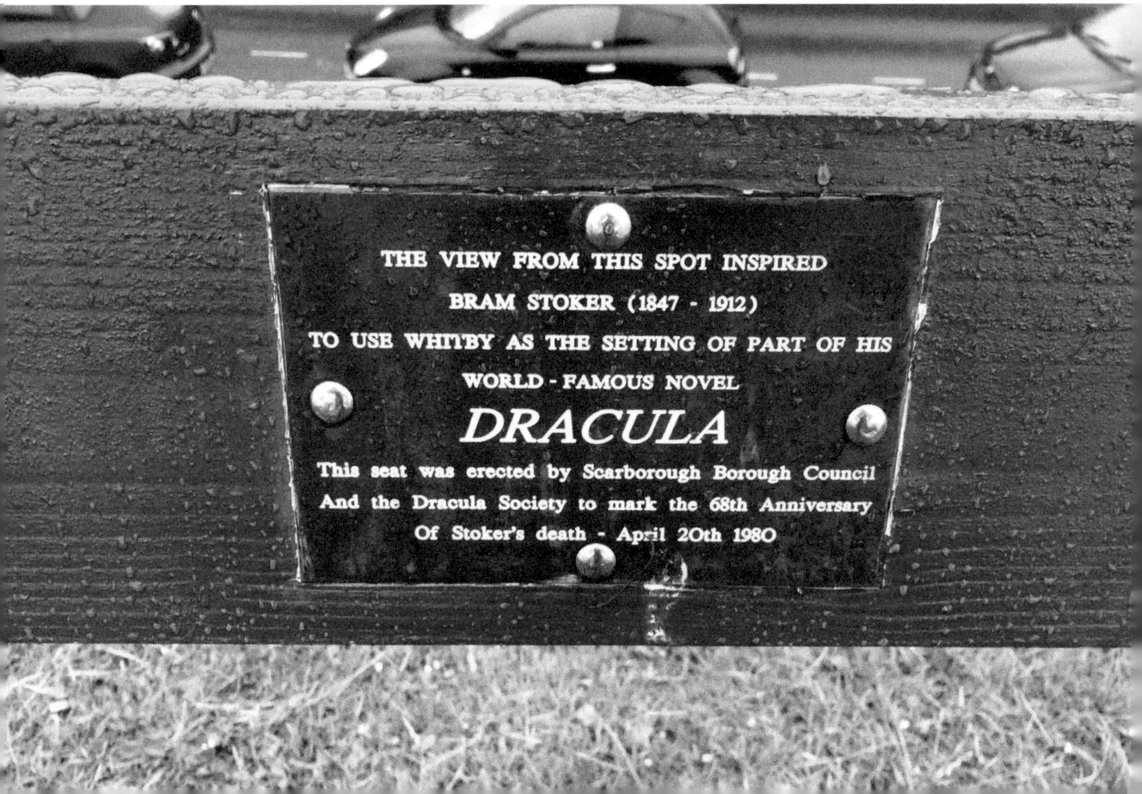

possible to stay in the very guest house where Bram Stoker lived during his holidays in Whitby and, if you visit No. 6 Royal Crescent, you can see the plaque commemorating Stoker. This quiet town house is where the world's most famous vampire was created.
See also: Authors, Dracula

Street Names

Whitby has a wealth of street names. It is not possible to mention them all, but a number of them are very old. Flowergate, for example, is mentioned in the Domesday Book of 1086, when Hugh, Earl of Chester, owned two carucates of land there. The name comes from 'Fiore', which in Latin and Italian is 'bloom, blossom, flower', or 'to adorn with flowers', so the name might have come about from the route (gate from 'gaeta', the Norse for a way or path) that may have passed through colourful land or fields.

Flowergate is on the West Cliff and, nearby, there is Baxtergate. A 'baxter' was a baker, so we can assume that it was here that bakers had their premises. In the Middle Ages, and for some time after, most people, especially if they lived in timber houses, could not bake their own bread. For that a stone building, with stone ovens, was needed.

Sandgate is another of the street names which retains the word 'gate'. The street gets its name because it was constructed near a sandy beach. A number of narrrow 'yards' come off Sandgate and used to lead to the beach.

Church Street used to be known as Kirkgate, 'the street where the church was'. The 199 Steps that lead to the abbey are on Church Lane, the continuation of Church Street, where there are several cottages dating to the fifteenth century. Also on Church Street is the Market Place and the Whitby Jet Heritage Centre.

Bridge Street is named after the swing bridge, built in Victorian times, that spans the River Esk. A replica of Captain Cook's ship *Endeavour* is moored nearby.
See also: Ghauts, Yards

Streonaeshalch

Streonaeshalch was how Whitby was known in Anglo-Saxon times. The Venerable Bede uses the name in *c.* 730 when he says that the name means 'bay of the lighthouse'. This feature, possibly of Roman origin, is believed to have stood at the top of the cliff on the east side of Whitby, near the abbey buildings. Other spellings include Streoneshalh, Streaneshalh, Strenaeshale and Streonesheaulh.

Another meaning for the name is 'fort bay', the place where the fort stood. Alternatively, the name might mean 'the corner of land, or halch, belonging to Streon, or Streona'. In this case, the original name of Whitby might refer to a person, Streon and Streona being plausible personal names. Or the place name might derive from a byname.

In Old English, Streon and Streona may derive from a word which means 'gain, profit or wealth'. In other words, the name might have been applied to the place because of how its development made someone quite wealthy. However, the spelling and the difficulty in pronouncing the word – especially if you were a French-speaking Norman – resulted in the name being changed to something that was easier to say.

Hwitebi might seem odd to us but it was from this word, clearly Danish in origin, that the modern name Whitby derives.

Sutcliffe, Frank Meadows

Frank Meadows Sutcliffe was not a Whitby man by birth. He was born in Headingley, near Leeds, in 1853, just at the time when photography was being developed as an art form. In 1871, he moved to Whitby, living at Bloomfield Terrace where he ran a portrait photography business at his studios in Skinner Street. Later he moved to the nearby village of Sleights, where he married and brought up a family.

In his spare time, he took photographs of ordinary people in Whitby building up, as he did so, a revealing picture of a Victorian seaside town and the people who lived and worked there. His photographs cover many, if not quite all, aspects of local life – the abbey, the harbour, fisher folk at work and at rest, children at play, street scenes in the town and he took many images of Robin Hood's Bay, Staithes, Runswick and Sandsend.

Sutcliffe's images of Whitby and its surrounding area make Whitby possibly the best documented Victorian town in England. Whereas other towns and cities might have good collections of postcard images, Whitby not only has this but also Frank Meadow Sutcliffe's images of the town and its people at home, at work and at play.

Synod of Whitby

The synod of 664 is, perhaps, the outstanding event to have taken place in Whitby. It was a council, held by King Oswiu of Northumbria, to establish unity of practice in the date of observing Easter and the style of tonsure within his kingdom.

At this time there were two traditions in Britain, the Celtic and the Roman, which differed on these and other issues. After hearing evidence from several sources, including St Hilda (see, Hilda, Saint) who supported the viewpoint of the Celts, Oswiu adopted the Roman practice. Those clergy who would not change withdrew to Iona and later to Ireland. Many historians claim that the synod had a profound effect on religious practices in England, but recent opinion suggests that the synod had little immediate impact outside Northumbria. However, both decisions were eventually adopted throughout England.

See also: Bede, Easter

T

Twin Cities

Most large towns are twinned with another and the reasons for this twinning are quite varied. For instance, the Scottish town of Dull is twinned with the Oregon town of Boring, playing on their amusing names. Sometimes towns will 'twin' because they have a shared connection and Whitby boasts seven! Anchorage in Alaska, Porirua in New Zealand, Stanley in the Falkland Islands, Whitby in Canada, Nuku'alofa in Tonga, Kauai County in Hawaii, and Osterode in Germany.

Many of these places had been visited by ships belonging to Captain Cook, such as Anchorage (where Cook named the Cook Inlet), Porirua (the harbour was mapped by Cook), Stanley (visited by Cook), Nuku'alofa (visited by Cook), and Kauai (visited by Cook). Whitby in Canada is named after Whitby when, in 1792, the surveyor in Canada named the townships east of Toronto after towns in north-east England. Osterode is technically twinned with the borough of Scarborough.

See also: Cook, Captain James

Whitby has many twin cities, mostly places visited by Captain Cook. This signpost on the West Cliff playfully points to some of Cook's destinations.

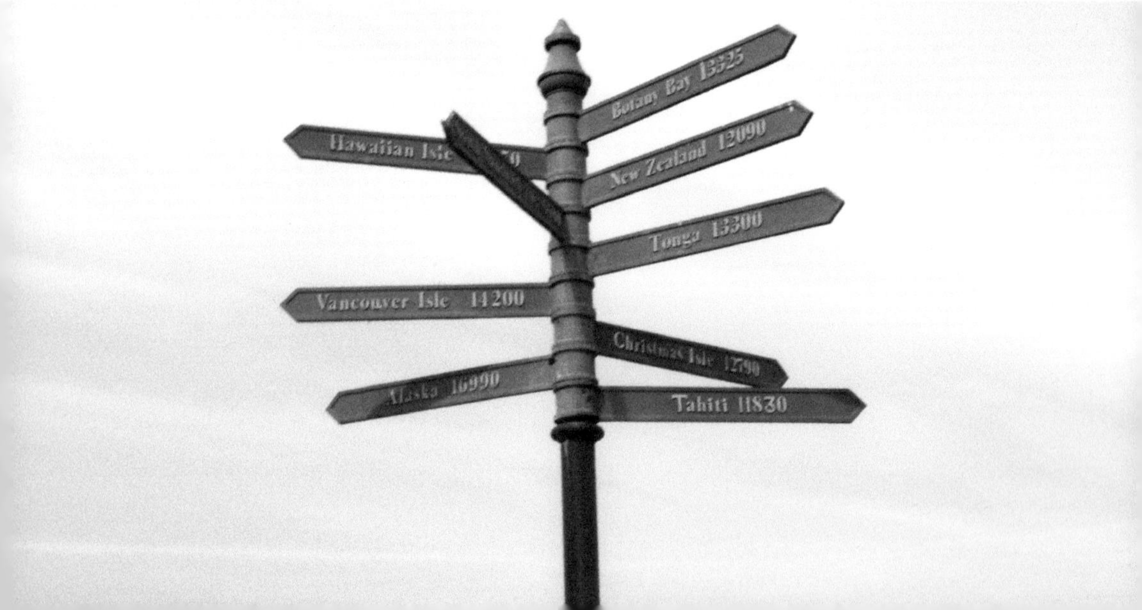

U

U-boats

During the First World War the waters off Whitby and Scarborough were dangerous places. At that time Britain relied on shipping for supplies to support the war effort and Germany was intent on disrupting this through battleship patrols, mines, and U-boats. Approximately 360 U-boats were launched by Germany and fought a war that is largely unknown to most people today.

Over 3,000 armed fishing vessels and 40,000 fishermen hunted down the U-boats in the waters around Great Britain. The coast off Whitby saw its fair share of action with at least five U-boats having been sunk in the area between Bridlington and Whitby. Two of these U-boats rest on the seabed close to Whitby. They are the UC70 (sunk on 28 August 1917) and the UB30 (sunk on 5 August 1918). These wrecks are classified as war graves as the submarines were lost with all the crew still on board.

The UC70 was a mine-laying submarine and had sunk thirty-three ships over a course of ten missions. On the day she was sunk, she had been spotted lying on the seabed close to Sandsend by a spotter plane, which directed the HMS *Ouse* to her location. The UC70 was depth-charged and sunk with the loss of all twenty-six of her crew.

The UB30 had been rammed by the armed trawler *John Gillman* and then subsequently attacked by shore batteries and depth charges before it too sank. The location of this submarine is kept secret to protect it from salvagers and trophy hunters and it too is classed as a war grave.

These are just a fraction of the hundreds of wrecks that lie off Whitby, either through conflict or accident, and reminds us of the danger that those who leave the harbour face on a daily basis.

See also: World War One Raid

V

Vikings

On 8 June 793 a shocking attack took place on the monastery of Lindisfarne by a Viking raiding party who saw the religious retreat as an easy target. For the Vikings, these were rich pickings as they contained great wealth and no weapons were turned against them.

Raids on English monasteries continued for seven decades, and in 866 the Vikings invaded East Anglia. After success there, they turned their attentions north. It is highly likely that the monastery at Whitby was destroyed during these Viking raids.

In November 866 the Vikings took York, a strong strategic position, and used it as their base to further establish their hold on England. In 875, Halfdan, one of the Viking leaders, seized the Midlands and was proclaimed the King of Northumbria. Land in the Derian province of Northumbria (which included all of Yorkshire and parts of Lancashire) was shared out among members of Halfdan's army.

Today the evidence of this is still apparent. Yorkshire was divided into three Ridings for the purpose of establishing military and political control. York remained outside of the Ridings to maintain impartiality. In addition, many settlements in Yorkshire show their Viking origins with the suffix 'by', which is an Old Norse term for settlement or farmstead, or 'wic', a dwelling, dwelling place, village, hamlet or town, the word coming from the Old English but borrowed from the Latin vicus.

Whitby became a Viking settlement and was known as Prestebi, meaning the 'settlement of priests' in Old Norse. This name was used in the eleventh century and was probably due to the re-establishment of the abbey in 1077–78 following the Norman Conquest. The town's name was recorded as Hwitebi and Witebi, meaning the 'white settlement' in Old Norse in the twelfth century, Whitebi in the thirteenth century, and Qwiteby in the fourteenth century, before finally becoming known as Whitby.

W

Whaling

Whitby was not the first town in England to become involved in the whaling industry, but it was eventually regarded as the capital of British whaling. The harbour was home to dozens of whalers. The ships, mostly built in Whitby, worked in the great Northern Fishery, in the North Atlantic, particularly around Greenland, though there were also whale fishing grounds off Canada and at Spitzbergen.

Among the first to exploit the Northern Fishery were the Basques from the Bay of Biscay, who were active from the sixteenth century. The Dutch, also in the sixteenth century, established a whaling industry in the ice-bound seas off Russia's northern coast. By the seventeenth century they had come to dominate that trade and retained great technical skill in the industry long after that.

So far as England was concerned, whaling was established by the newly created Muscovy Company, founded in 1555 in London. Over a century later the English took advantage of the political situation in Holland, particularly after 1660, to extend their industry and London joined other coastal towns in both England and Scotland who established whaling fisheries of their own.

Whaling in Hull can be traced back to 1598. Whitby became involved in 1753, when the Whitby Whaling Co. was set up. At around the same time a group of other towns on the east coast, including Newcastle, Sunderland and Scarborough, also became involved. They took advantage of a sudden increase in demand for the products associated with the whale at the time when the Industrial Revolution was gathering pace. As the latter progressed the whaling industry expanded and the profits that could be made from it grew rapidly.

The main product obtained from the whale was oil, which was in great demand in the wool industry of Yorkshire and the increasingly important Lancashire cotton industry. The oil was obtained from the blubber of the whale and, from it, oil for the textile industry, soap, margarine, paint, candles and lubricants were made. It is often forgotten that, before gas street lighting, whale oil lamps were used. The skin of the whale was made into leather and the cartilage of the animal was made into glue.

It was not only whales that Whitby men fished for. It has been estimated that, over the years of the Whitby whaling industry (1753–*c.* 1837), some 25,000 seals, 2,761

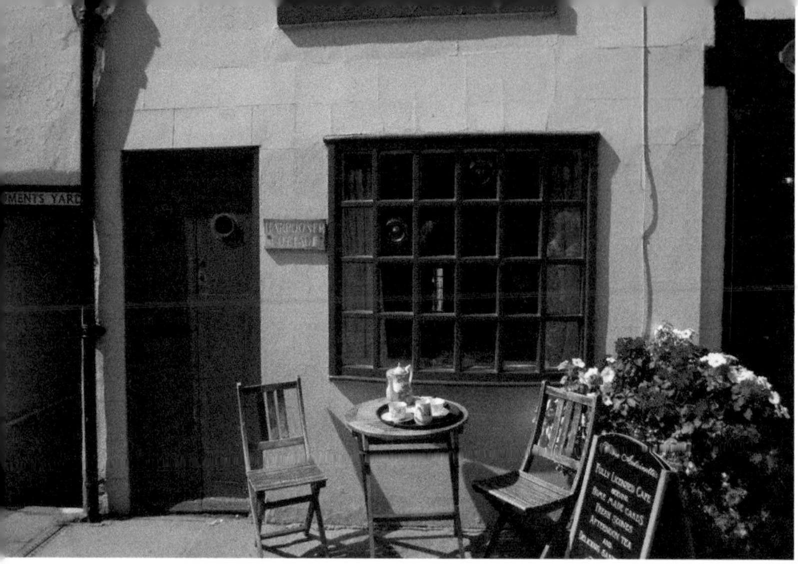

Harpooner Cottage on the east side of Whitby hints at the town's whaling history.

whales and fifty-five polar bears were captured and brought back to Whitby for processing.

The whaling industry was important to Whitby because it led to other industries being established in the town. Shipbuilding was one, and, though Whitby built more colliers for the coastal coal trade, it is recorded that between 1753 and 1833, fifty-three whalers operated in Whitby. Where there were shipbuilders, there were also makers of rope, sailcloth and importers of timber and other products that were necessary.

Boiler houses were established around the harbour. They turned whale blubber into oil in an unpleasant industry, which, to some, made the harbour something of a no-go area.

Fortunes were made in the Whitby whaling industry. Of the families that became prominent because of their involvement, the Scoresby's – father and son, both called William – are the most well-known. William (Senior) is accredited with the invention of the Crow's Nest and he also brought back to Whitby the largest single catch recorded. His son, William Junior, was a prominent explorer. It was he who discovered that sea temperatures, at depth, were much warmer than at the surface. Similarly, he worked on how iron affected the use of the compass and terrestrial magnetism.

The success of the whaling families led to the development of the West Cliff, where they built large houses. They were joined by other families, many of whom had made their money from whaling or from industries related to whaling.

Whale Jaw

The whale jaw arch on the West Cliff is one of Whitby's most well-known landmarks. In the past jawbones of a whale would be attached to the mast of a whaler to let investors know that the voyage being completed had been a success. The present arch dates from 1963 when Whitby RDC accepted a gift from Thor Dhal and artist Graham Leach to record Whitby's whaling past. The bones were replaced in 2002 as a gift from Whitby's twin town of Anchorage in Alaska.

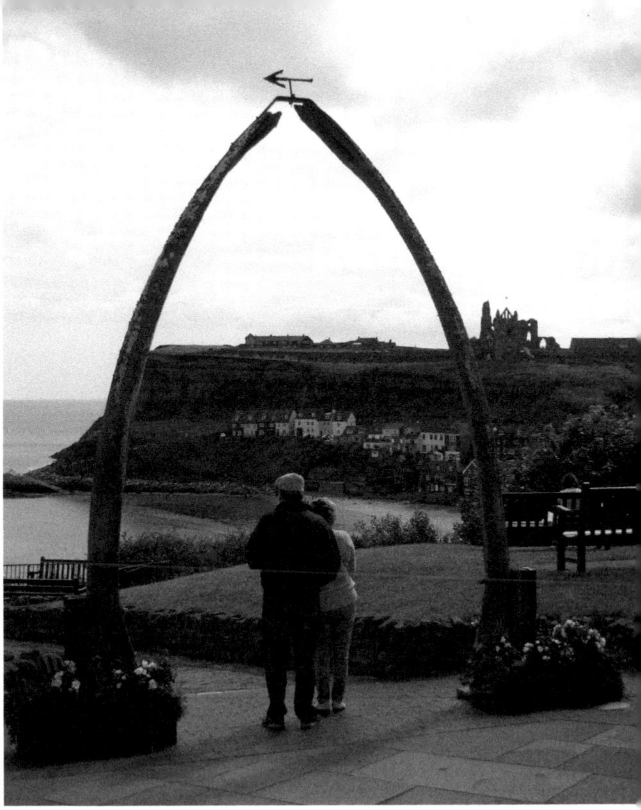

An arch made from the jawbones of whales had stood at the edge of the West Cliff for many years. The Whalebone Arch remains a popular place for a photograph in Whitby.

Whitby Cat

A 'Whitby Cat' is a shallow draught, lightly rigged vessel built in Whitby for the coastal trade. The name literally means 'coal and timber ship', a ship which carried coal from the north-east of England to London, returning to Whitby with cargoes of timber. Whitby made a large number of these vessels, which were based on Norwegian predecessors. They were popularised by Captain Cook during his voyages of discovery.

Whitby Hall

Whitby Hall, otherwise known as Abbey House or Cholmley Hall, stands on the site of the Abbot's House, or Lodging, at Whitby Abbey. The building was erected by Sir Francis Cholmley in *c.* 1580, using stones from the abbey. It was enlarged by Sir Hugh Cholmley in 1635 and, during the English Civil War, the property was fortified and garrisoned by Royalist forces. This, however, did not prevent the building being taken by Parliamentary forces. Sir Hugh had resisted Parliamentary attacks at Scarborough Castle for a year and the taking of the hall was in reprisal for this.

Other additions to the hall were made by later members of the Cholmley family in the seventeenth century and it remained in their hands until the later eighteenth century when the family moved to Howsham Hall in the village of that name, near Malton in North Yorkshire.

Whitby Hall was not lived in for some time and, early in the nineteenth century, part of it was damaged in a storm. The building was then abandoned but, in the later nineteenth century, the building was renovated by Sir C. W. Strickland who lived there for part of the year.

Whitby Whale

A 'Whitby Whale' is a term for a large serving of fish in a fish and chip shop. It is a phrase that is not only alliterative but is comes from Whitby's former association with the whaling industry. Some say that the fish and chips served in the town's seventeen or eighteen fish and chips shops are the best in Britain. It would be invidious to mention one firm but the Magpie Café on the West Cliff and Hadley's on the East Cliff are perhaps the best known, though all the Whitby fish and chips eaten by the authors of this book have been pretty amazing.

William of Topcliffe

William, 1st Baron of Topcliffe, otherwise William de Percy, became intimately involved in the history of Whitby. He was born *c.* 1034, probably at the family fief of Perci, near Villedieu, on the Cotentin Peninsula in Normandy. It is possible that he settled in England before the Norman Conquest, possibly at the invitation of Edward the Confessor, but he was not welcome there when Harold II came to the throne. It is likely that William de Percy returned to Normandy and was not with the Conqueror at Hastings.

The cartulary of Whitby Abbey states that de Percy was back in the country in 1067. He was with the king, who had returned to Normandy, and Hugh de Avranches, the Earl Hugh mentioned in the Domesday Book, of whom William de Percy was a follower and great friend.

In 1070 we find William de Percy at York working on the repair at the castle after it had been destroyed by the Danes, and in 1072, he accompanied the king on his Scottish campaign. At this time, it is likely that de Percy joined his friend de Avranches in the Harrying of the North, which brought the northern parts of the country back under the Conqueror's control. The latter was rewarded with the great Earldom of Chester for his services. This included the great Lordship of Whitby, which Hugh granted to William.

So, by 1086, William de Percy was tenant in chief, with 118 manors in the three Ridings of Yorkshire. He also had significant estates in Lindsey, in Lincolnshire, and other lands in Nottinghamshire and Hampshire. These latter were brought to him by his English wife, Emma de Porte.

It was William who refounded Whitby Abbey in *c.* 1077, appointing Serlo, his brother, the first abbot. He built the castle at Topcliffe and joined Robert Curthose, Duke of Normandy, on the First Crusade, where he died. He was buried at Antioch in *c.* 1096, but his heart was brought back to England and buried at Whitby Abbey.

William of Topcliffe, as he became known, was the founder of the great Percy family, who, in later centuries, moved their interests to Northumberland.

See also: Hugh, Earl of Chester

World War One Raid

On 16 December 1914 the German navy launched a devastating attack on the ports of Hartlepool, Scarborough and Whitby. There were 592 casualties during the raid, of which 137 were fatalities.

At 8 a.m. the German Battlecruisers *Derfflinger* and *Von der Tann* started to attack Scarborough, hitting the castle, Grand Hotel and several other properties, before moving up the coast to Whitby at 9:30 a.m. Just off the coast, the two cruisers began to shell Whitby, attempting to hit the coastguard station on the East Cliff. Whitby Abbey was also hit and damaged during the bombardment along with several other properties. Following the attack, the German ships fled through a minefield that their own fleet had laid to deter any pursuit.

The attack caused great public outcry and was used as a propaganda tool to encourage men to enlist in the British army and avenge those killed and injured in the attack. The slogan 'Remember Scarborough' was often used in recruiting campaigns during the war.

In Whitby today there is a memorial garden on the West Cliff which commemorates the attack. It shows a replica of a destroyed house as a result of the bombardment.

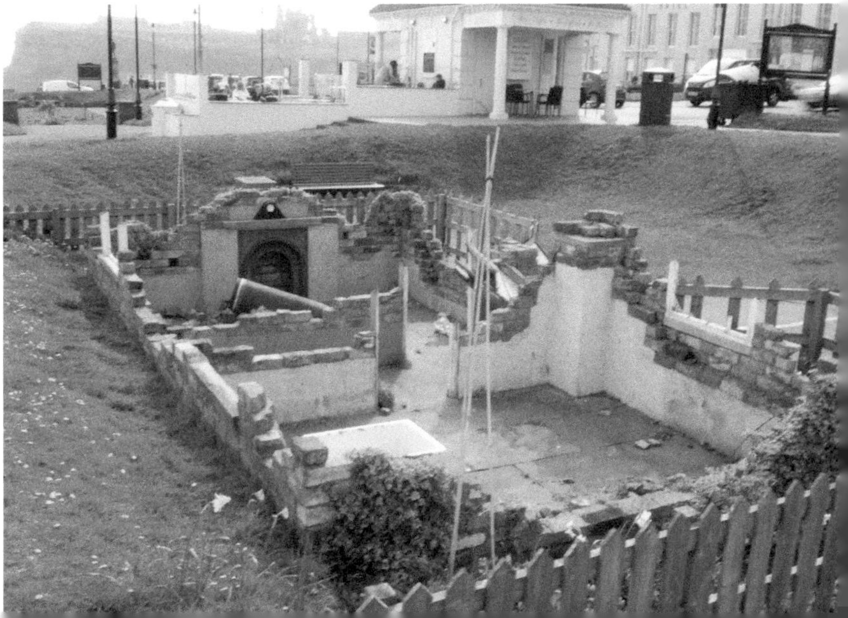

This memorial is designed to replicate a home damaged in the famous raid on Whitby during the First World War.

Y

Yards

One of the most remarkable features of Whitby is the survival of many of its 'yards'. These are the narrow alleyways and ghauts, but mostly known as yards, which exist in both the old and the newer parts of town. It has been estimated that, at one time, there must have been over 200 of them, of which some eighty still survive.

The yards can be traced to the Middle Ages when narrow strips of property, on what were then the main streets, were sold off or leased for development. These strips of land were known as burgages, a tenure in socage for a yearly rent.

At the short end, and on an existing street – Sandgate, off Bridge Street, is a good example – a house, a shop or an inn might be built, the long, narrow property behind being used as gardens or sites for stables or workshops. In time these narrow strips of land would be developed, mostly for housing, by the family that owned the property on the street. Alternatively, small plots of land might be sold off for someone else to build a cottage, or, perhaps several cottages.

In the past, yards where often dirty, lacking in hygienic facilities and overcrowded. In some cases, thirty to forty families might live in these conditions but, in more recent times, some of the yards have become very attractive places in which to live, some with their own gardens. The latter have sometimes been made when old property has been pulled down, particularly in government-sponsored schemes in the 1930s, and not built on, residents claiming the right to make gardens on the sites of former cottages.

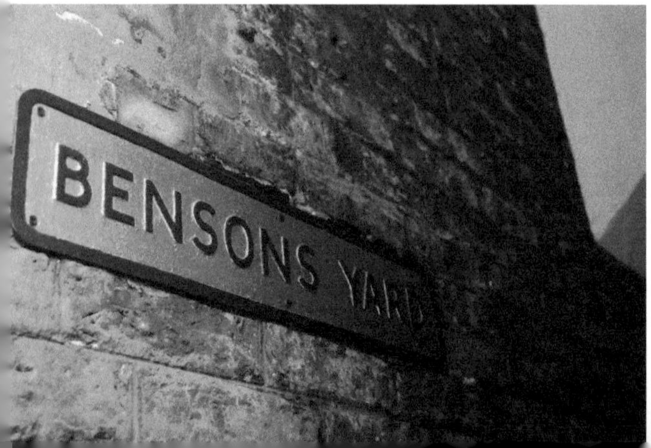

Bensons Yard in Whitby. The yards of Whitby once numbered over 200; now only around eighty remain.

Yards are accessed by narrow paths, some of which are open to the public. Others are private and this privacy should be respected. A number are 'through' yards in that they have a front entrance and a rear exit.

The names of these yards, and their history, have been the subject of several publications, the most recent of which is Alan Whitworth's *Whitby Yards Through Time* (Amberley, 2012). However, the most famous name is that of Argument's Yard, of which there were two, one off Church Street, the other off the Cragg (now demolished). It has been speculated that the name derives from a political debate that once took place there. This is unlikely and the name may have come from an Anglicisation of the Flemish name Argoment.

Other 'yards' are named after specific buildings (Custom House Yard, Bakehouse Yard, Friends Meeting House Yard and Queen's Hotel Yard) but others seem to be named after the families who might have developed them. There is a yard known as Dark Entry Yard, which may not have sinister origins – but, remember, this is Whitby!

See also: Ghauts, Street Names

Below left: The yards appear to be small dark alleyways but, in some instances, open into beautiful spaces.

Below right: The famous Arguments Yard in Whitby. But what does its name really mean?

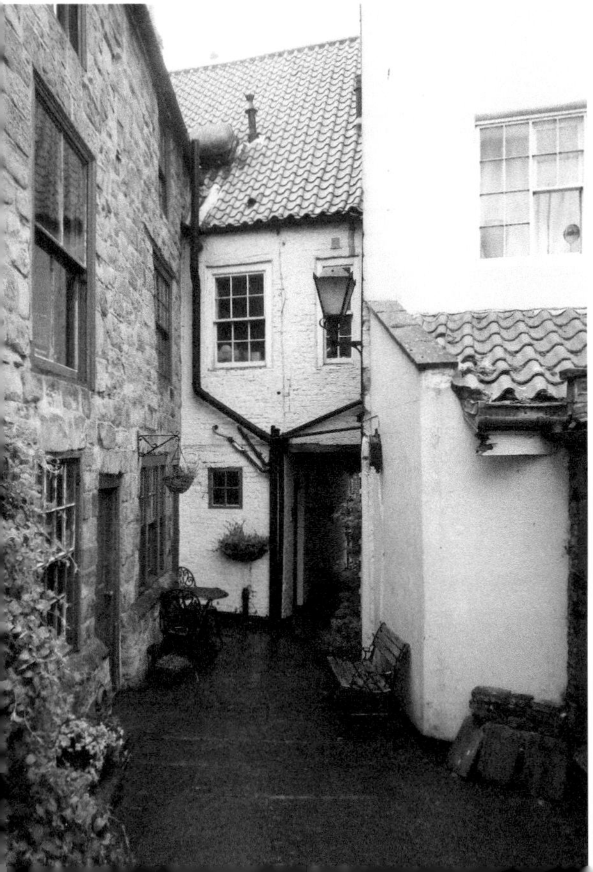

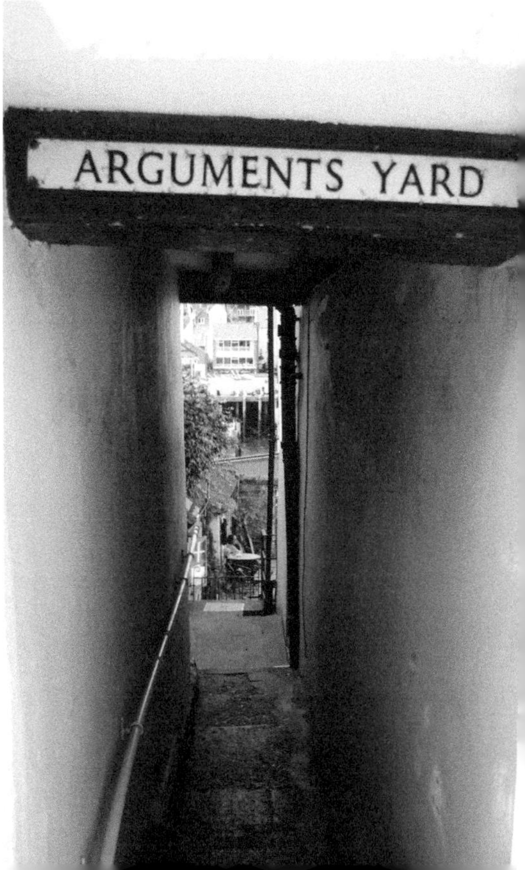

Z

Zig Zag

The Zig Zag is a meandering path that leads to the large beach beneath the West Cliff. It also allows holidaymakers an easy route from their lodgings to the brightly coloured beach huts on the narrow promenade at the edge of the beach. It can be found close to the Pavilion and is ideal for those who just want to laze about on the beach and watch the world go by.

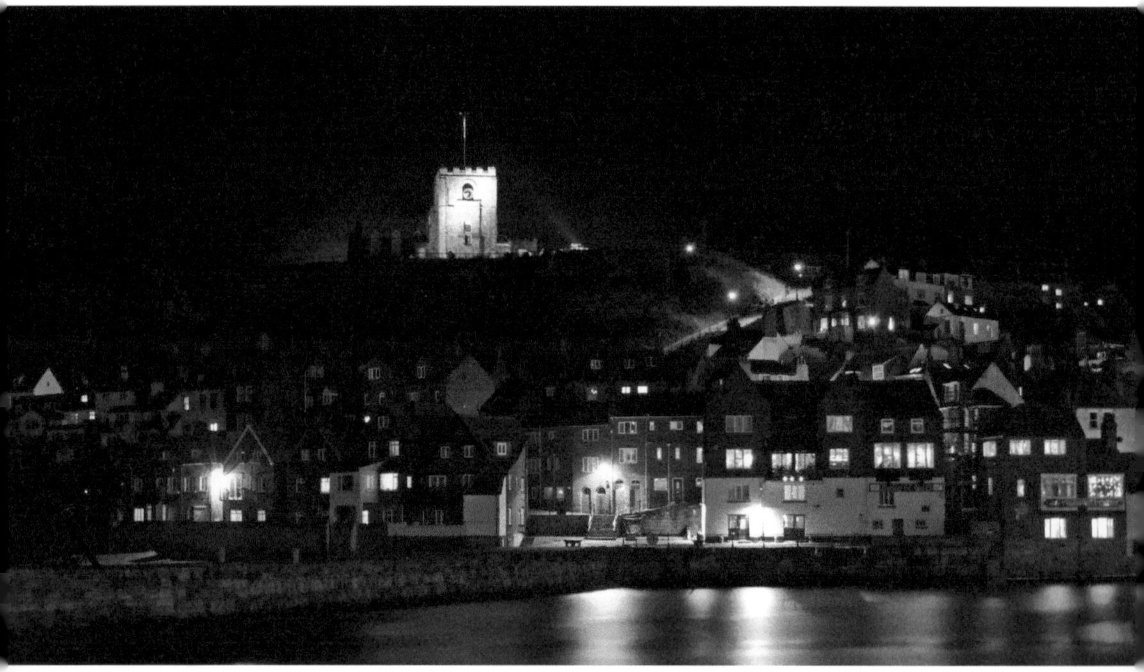

Whitby at night. The town loses none of its beauty even when the sun goes down.